The Ride Delegate

The Ride Delegate

MEMOIR OF A WALT DISNEY
WORLD VIP TOUR GUIDE

Annie Salisbury

Theme Park Press

© 2014 ANNIE SALISBURY

No part of this publication may be reproduced, distributed, or transmitted in any form or by any means, including photocopying, recording, or other electronic or mechanical methods, without the prior written permission of the publisher, except for brief quotations embodied in critical reviews and certain other noncommercial uses permitted by copyright law.

Although every precaution has been taken to verify the accuracy of the information contained herein, no responsibility is assumed for any errors or omissions, and no liability is assumed for damages that may result from the use of this information.

Theme Park Press is not associated with the Walt Disney Company, the Disney Family, or any of the individuals or companies associated with either or both of them.

The views expressed in this book are those of the author alone.

Theme Park Press publishes its books in a variety of print and electronic formats. Some content that appears in one format may not appear in another.

Editor: Bob McLain
Layout: Artisanal Text

ISBN 978-1-941500-09-5
Printed in the United States of America

Theme Park Press | www.ThemeParkPress.com
Address queries to bob@themeparkpress.com

According to Disney Legend, this is all true.

GLOSSARY OF TERMS

Tour Guide: Synonymous with "always looks tired".

Tour Coordinator: The Gary Sinese of VIP tours.

DSA: Disney Special Activities. The fancy term for the Tour Office.

Tour Office, or just Office: Where the tour magic happens. Central command.

Every Other Coordinator on Disney Property: The second line of defense after a regular Cast Member.

Manager: In charge. Always has at least two phones and a metal trash picker. Sometimes helpful, sometimes not helpful, always judging.

FastPass: A reservation ticket to experience an attraction at a designated time with little to no wait in the return queue. RIP: 1995–2014. Predecessor to FastPass+.

Greeter: The person who stands outside the attraction and waves hello to everyone. Usually in charge of checking FastPass return times.

Merge: Cast Member at the point where FastPass and the standby line come together.

Grouper: The person who assigns designated seating locations on attractions for guests. Usually looks frazzled.

The Bridge: The Liberty Square Bridge in Liberty Square where there are actually seats to watch the parade. Designated VIP viewing unless otherwise noted.

Park One: The parking lot located directly behind Main Street (on Tony's side). The one and only allowed parking location in Magic Kingdom.

Dining Card: My ticket to eat a million corn dog nuggets.

Premium Tour: The tour for your Next Door Neighbor.

PEP Tour: The tour for Tom Cruise and his family.

PEPing: The art of going in the back entrance of an attraction with Tom Cruise and his family.

PROLOGUE

I was sixteen and sitting in the Beach Club lobby crying *hysterically*. I was crying so heavily that my entire family started to distance themselves from me, with Dad moving to the checkout counter to end our hotel stay, and Mom becoming very interested in the artist doing portraits in the far corner. Even my sisters, ages fourteen and six, didn't want anything to do with me, as they both slowly drifted apart from this hysterical teenager, now causing a ruckus in a very upscale Disney deluxe hotel.

Why was I crying hysterically? Because Dad had just informed my sisters and I that this was our last Disney World trip *ever*.

"Say goodbye to Disney World," were his exact words. "You'll see this place again when you pay for your own family to visit."

That's when I broke out into hysterical tears.

My sisters took the news like well-adjusted children and nodded with Dad's words. Meanwhile, I was all like, blubbering mess, incoherent gibberish, *why would you do this to me*??

At age sixteen I thought I still had a few more Disney trips in me before I was set into the "real world". I couldn't understand why my parents weren't already planning next year's Disney trip, like they sometimes did during the current trip. It saved some money, and if you know anything about Disney you know that it's expensive. Why would they want to pass up another family vacation like this? Where were we going to go on vacation next year? I didn't understand.

My parents wanted to try a new destination, and kept on suggesting places like Europe, and I'd groan and moan and proclaim, "Isn't that what EPCOT is for?" like the teenager I was back then.

Whether I agreed with it or not, the thought that I wouldn't come back to Disney World slowly started to sink in, and I sat on the couch in the Beach Club lobby with my knees pulled into my chest and sobbed. At age sixteen I had just discovered the wonders of mascara, and I knew that thick black runny lines were streaming down my face. I was wearing black gym shorts and a blue shirt that said TENNIS across the front of it, like a proclamation that at one point in gym class I had probably played tennis.

An older gentleman slowly started to approach my fetal position on the couch, and I looked up through teary eyes to see who it was. It was the Beach Club lobby greeter, a man by the name of Art. He was the quintessential Southern gentleman and if he told me the ocean was made of jell-o I would have believed him. He was always standing in the lobby when we came back from the parks, all tired and sweaty, but *he* was always chipper and friendly, tipping his white sailor hat to us and calling me "princess".

"What's wrong, princess?" he kneeled down to my level and pulled a handkerchief out of one of his pockets. Of course he had a handkerchief on hand, just in case there was a manic child in his presence.

"My Dad [sniff] says we're never [sob sob sob] coming [hiccup] back to [deep breath] Disney World!" I managed to say to him, though I bet it was nothing less than incoherent. Art understood, though, and he patted my shoulder like he was everyone's grandfather.

"Don't cry, princess! You can always come back to Disney World!"

I stopped crying. I don't know what resonated with Art's words, but it was like I knew that he was right. It was like he was a magical sage, Grandmother Willow, The Blue Fairy, Edna Mode, Rafiki, and Gusteau, all wrapped into one, and I believed his words wholeheartedly. I used his handkerchief to dab my tears, and handed him back a mascara stained white square of fabric. He chuckled.

"Disney World will always be here for you. You'll come back." He had a twinkle in his eye and I bet that if he had snapped his fingers at that exact moment, he would have disappeared in a cloud of smoke like the best soothing Disney animatronic you've ever seen.

If only Art knew how right he had been.

Eleven minutes. That's how long I have before my guests would get off of Jungle Cruise. I ushered them towards the waiting boat ahead of me, making sure that all of them stepped down into the vessel leaving me behind on the dock. That's a little trick I had learned over time—make sure all of the guests get on first. That way, if you decide at the last moment to slip away there is literally nothing they can to do stop you, because they are fastened under their restraints and you're standing at the loading dock waving goodbye.

"You're not riding?" a skipper asks me.

I smiled as wide as I could, and through gritted teeth told him, "Not today!" I looked at my watch. Eleven minutes.

I didn't have time to watch my guests disappear around the corner on the boat. They were seated inside of the ride vehicle and I was free for eleven minutes. They had already forgotten about me, because they were about to ride a ride! I darted between the skippers standing on the dock and made my way past the queue towards the unloading area. There was a rope net tucked off to the side that separated the onstage world from the backstage world, and I ducked behind it. I looked at my watch. Freedom for ten more minutes.

Picking up my pace, I hurried down the pathway, past Cast Members smoking, past the Jungle Cruise makeshift break area (which was really just a hut with lockers, a sad excuse for a fan, and a water cooler), and into the Jungle Cruise maintenance area. A bottomless hippo laughed at me as I raced up the incline that would take me to Main Street, behind the Emporium, behind the fire station, behind City Hall. Someone yelled hello to me as I walked past, and I threw my hand up over my head to signal that I had heard them, but I honestly didn't have time for them right now. I had ten minutes and I had to pee.

I pushed open the backstage door to City Hall and then pushed through another door into the women's restroom, where I unloaded my belongings and took my phones out of my pockets and threw my black purse onto the counter. I should have a water bottle with me, but I had lost that somewhere earlier in the day and I just hadn't gotten around to buying a new one. I needed a new one; that's why I had to pee, anyway. It was hot as blazes in the park today and I knew how much fun it was to become dehydrated on a tour, and I couldn't deal with that strife again. Whenever I had a free second, I bought and chugged as much water as possible. I wish I could say that my water consumption was helping with my skin complexion, but I was wearing so much sunscreen and foundation with sunscreen and oil-controlling powder it was a miracle that my entire face wasn't encased in zits. The hot summer sun was not helping anything regarding my face.

As I washed my hands, I looked at myself in the mirror. Even I knew I looked tired, and I had gotten a solid seven hours of sleep last night. Was it the sun? Was the sun eating away at my face, making it look like I had been up for days? Was it the fact that I hadn't eaten anything substantial today, aside from two pretzels in the shape of Mickey Mouse? Was it because I hadn't had a day off in thirteen days, and still wouldn't have one off for four more? Was I just perpetually tired all of the time now?

6   The Ride Delegate

Eight minutes. I didn't have time to think about this stuff now.

I raced back to Jungle Cruise, now walking so fast I might have been running. My feet hurt with every step because I had worn through another pair of shoes, yet again, and the soles on these no longer functioned as anything other than a thin piece of fabric keeping me off of the hot black sidewalk. I needed new shoes, but I honestly didn't have the money to go and buy them. Maybe if these guests thanked me well enough today, I could take $20 and go to Wal-Mart and buy another cheap pair to get me through the rest of the month. I just needed a pair to last me a few more weeks. Then I would have time to research and purchase brand-new, comfortable shoes that wouldn't destroy my feet.

I pushed back the rope net and appeared onstage at the exit of Jungle Cruise. I looked at my watch. Seven minutes. I was making pretty good time today. I looked towards the unload area, where the boats would come into dock, and I could see that two boats away was the wheelchair boat. That would buy me at least another three minutes; I knew the Cast Members had to unload one wheelchair before they could load another. I was so hungry. I had already peed, could I really push my luck and get something to eat, too?

The Jungle Cruise area is crowded, because of course it's always crowded. I don't know why someone thought it would be a good idea to place so many things on top of one another in Adventureland, but I wasn't invited to that meeting way back when. Jungle Cruise sat at the bottom of a hill, and I knew at the top of the hill there was a tiny little food cart that had the best eggrolls, and the only eggrolls, in the park. The eggrolls were delicious. They were like hung-over greasy food and that's all I could think about right now. I ran up the hill, darting between strollers and wheelchairs and guests mulling about like they didn't have anything better to do with their time besides stand right in the middle of a walkway in Adventureland.

There was a line for the eggrolls, because of course there was. It was just after 2pm in the afternoon so everyone in the Magic Kingdom was suddenly like, "we should totally get eggrolls in Adventureland." It was about four guests deep, but I was so hungry. I looked at my watch. Five minutes. Plus the time of the wheelchair boat to unload, and then reload. So maybe eight minutes, tops. That's all I could allow myself.

I placed myself at the end of the eggroll line. There was a kid and his mother standing in front of me, and the kid tugged on his mom's sleeve and looked at me, confused, like I might yell at him for something he had done earlier somewhere in the park. The mother turned around to look at me. "Do you need to get by?" she asked, confused, since guests were always confused to see Cast Members freely roaming the park like I did so often.

"No, I'm hungry just like you!" I laughed, through gritted teeth, and prayed that this wouldn't take long.

After what felt like forever, I reached the front of the eggroll line. I just wanted an eggroll. I looked into the eggroll case, and saw that there were no eggrolls left, only corn dogs. Whatever. I needed something to eat. "One corn dog, please," I said to the Cast Member behind the counter, handing him my company-issued ID.

The Cast Member took my ID and looked at it. "No Cast Member discount," he said.

"I know," I replied, "One corn dog, please."

The Cast Member looked at my ID picture, and then he looked at me. I knew that he had no idea what was going on. This Cast Member could not figure out why I, a Guest Relations Cast Member, was standing in front of him, clad in full costume, asking for a corn dog.

"I can't take your dining discount here," he said again.

"Do you know how to work a dining *card*?" I knew that my tone was harsh, and I didn't mean for it to be. It was just bothersome that many Cast Members in the park looked at me like I must be crazy. I was not, in fact, crazy, I was just hungry, and tired, and hot, and cranky, and my guests were getting off of Jungle Cruise in less than three minutes and I needed to eat something.

The Cast Member shook his head. He didn't know how to work a dining card.

"I can walk you through the whole thing. One corn dog, please. And a bottle of water. Then, hit total. In the bottom left hand corner of your screen you'll see a button that says, 'VIP TOUR DISCOUNT'. Hit that button. You'll be prompted to swipe my ID. And just like magic, you'll get two receipts and I'll sign yours!" I had given that spiel so many time I was honestly surprised every time I met someone in Food and Beverage that didn't know how to work a dining card. Like, are you new, kid?

Something clicked in the Cast Member's mind, and like a bolt of lighting he had figured out who I was, and what role I was performing, and what I was doing, and just how hungry I was. Oh, a VIP dining card! But instead this guy said, "Oh, the system's actually down. Cash only."

I grunted, out loud, like I sometimes do when something really irks me. I was so hungry. I was thirsty. I had two minutes now to eat something and get back to Jungle Cruise before my guests got off of the attraction, if they weren't off already. Sometimes that was the most embarrassing thing, to have guests disembark from the ride and not be standing there waiting for them. In this business, time is money.

The corn dog was staring me right in the face. I needed to eat it. Without thinking twice I reached into my purse and pulled out my wallet. I knew I had cash, I just didn't really want to break the cash I had on me, which happened to be the "stickers" (tips) from the guests I had hosted the day before. "Can you break a $50?" I asked him, though it was really more of a command than an inquiry.

I shoved the change back into my bag, and with my corn dog and water in hand, I raced down to the exit of Jungle Cruise. I didn't see my guests waiting there, so I probably had about thirty seconds to wolf down the entire corn dog, give or take. And boy, did I go to town on that corn dog, barely even registering that it was piping hot still, and it was a thousand degrees outside, and I was completely burning the roof of my mouth as I chewed furiously on it, but I was hungry and that's all that mattered. I wonder how many guests looked over at me as I ate that corn dog at the exit of Jungle Cruise. I wonder what any of them thought. Did they think, look at that poised and proper VIP Tour Guide delicately eat that hot dog deep-fried on a stick? Or did they think, that Cast Member needs to be put out of her misery in a backstage location? Did they turn to their son or daughter and say, sweetie, you should aspire to be a Tour Guide so you can eat corn dogs at the exit of Jungle Cruise, too. Or did they just pity me. Pity the tour guide who was so hungry she made the bold decision to eat something on a stick in clear guest view because why not.

I know what I thought. I thought, my god, what life decisions have I made thus far to boil down to the fact that I am eating a corn dog, in full costume, on the clock, at the exit of Jungle Cruise?

ONE

The first time I visited Walt Disney World I was one-and-a-half years old, and according to my parents, trashcans, water fountains, and butter in the shape of Mickey Mouse fascinated me. Not a whole lot has changed. My mom, dad, and I stayed at Caribbean Beach, and it was during this vacation they learned that I suffered from horrible motion sickness because we needed to take a bus everywhere. Every day my mom dressed me in one outfit, and then by the time we reached our destination, she needed to change me into another one. We never stayed at Caribbean Beach again. From there on in it was Beach Club or bust. Before I turned eighteen I had visited Disney World sixteen times.

Every August it was customary for my family to head to Disney. I knew some of my friends found this tradition odd, because my family never went to the beach and we never took cross country road trips in an RV like so many of them did. We traded our beach vacation for Stormalong Bay, and we were all fine with that. My sisters and I all learned to swim in the kiddie pool there. I hated the way real sand felt in my hands because I was so conditioned to the artificial sand lining the bottom of that pool.

I lived and breathed everything Disney. Looking around my childhood bedroom you'll find it completely cluttered with Disney knick-knacks and toys. There's a crate of old park maps underneath my bed. I always had a current Disney World map right above my desk, so I could sit and do homework and stare at all the places I could visit in Magic Kingdom. I'd think about being in Disney World and my heart would literally long to be there. I had never felt such longing for a thing or a place before. I had an iTunes folder just full of Disney theme music. All I have to do is hear a few bars of "Moonlight Serenade", and instantly I would be transported back to Hollywood Boulevard in Hollywood Studios. When I smelled dry ice I thought of riding Winnie the Pooh. I cleaned my fish tank when it finally started to smell like the Living Seas. I found myself planning vacations for friends, with detailed itineraries and the best places to eat across property. At age 15, I was already a lexicon of Disney information.

As we walked through the park, my family used to joke about the perfect Disney job. We had conflicting ideas, since my mom wanted to work in the Emporium on Main Street and my youngest sister wanted to be a "Disney World vet" (this discussion happened pre-Animal Kingdom, when that dream became a reality). I just wanted to work at the Haunted Mansion, as the person who opened the doors to the attraction and told everyone to move into the dead center of the room. That seemed like the perfect job for me.

Years went by and every year we went to Disney. There was one summer when my mom was pregnant with my littlest sister, and the family went to Canada instead, and the middle sister and I complained that there weren't "any rides". I couldn't comprehend a vacation without queues and fireworks and churros. There was also one year when my parents suggested we stay off Disney property at a timeshare in Orlando, and my sisters and I scoffed at the idea so much, my parents canceled the vacation. We didn't go to Disney that year, either.

My post-college plans fell apart during the spring semester of my senior year and I no longer had a job. I didn't have anything else lined up, and I needed to do something with my shiny new bachelor of science degree in communications. I started thinking about all of those Disney trips that my family had taken, and about how I had always wanted to be the person who opened the doors at Haunted Mansion, and I figured I didn't have anything to lose. My mom always talked about how she and my dad regretted never being Cast Members for a short period of time after they were married. But then they had me, and they couldn't just pick up and move to Orlando for the fun of it. I could.

I remember sitting in my tiny dorm room applying for the Disney College Program. I'll always remember the senior seminar I was sitting in when my acceptance email for the College Program came through. I burst out of the lecture hall and called my mom, yelling into the phone that I was going to work at Haunted Mansion and my dreams were finally coming true. I wondered if I could stay at Disney forever, but that idea still seemed so far down the road. I told myself I'd stay until the magic wore off. Then I'd have to leave.

Flash-forward six months, and I was not assigned to work Haunted Mansion. Instead, I was assigned to work attractions at DisneyQuest. I wanted to leave. It was not magical.

DisneyQuest. The only attraction not in a park. The first few months of my college program are sort of a blur, because I cried a whole lot. I was devastated to be placed at DisneyQuest. I couldn't understand how Disney could do that to me. Didn't they know who I was? Didn't they know that I had spent my whole life dreaming of working in a park, opening doors at the Haunted Mansion, directing parades, and collecting FastPasses? I had spent the entire summer leading up to my Disney immigration pretending to call through a queue line for a "party of two"!

I begged anyone who would listen to let me transfer roles. The thing about being a CP is that you can't transfer roles no matter how many times you cry in your homeroom manager's office. I really do owe a lot to the managers I had at DisneyQuest, because they helped me stop crying. They showed me that working at DisneyQuest wasn't that bad, because I was out of the building every day by 11:30pm at the latest. They reminded me that I could be working in Magic Kingdom and pulling all-nighters for Extra Magic Hours. This was true. I did not want to be standing in Magic Kingdom at 3am. After a few months, I stopped crying and I learned to love DisneyQuest. That was my first Disney home.

I couldn't stay at DisneyQuest forever, though. As my college program started winding down, my mom began asking me what I was going to do next. I figured I would stay at Disney, because it wasn't like I had anything else lined up to do. Besides, I liked my job, I liked my friends, and I was having fun spending every waking moment hanging out at the parks. Disney World was my playground. I had free admission and I didn't buy groceries so I could eat Casey's Corner corn dog nuggets, my guilty pleasure and comfort food all rolled into one. When my program ended, I moved into an apartment in Orlando.

My managers at DisneyQuest suggested that I apply for Guest Relations. They thought I had the personality, and the thick skin, to be in a role like that. On a whim I applied, and a month later I found myself sitting in an interview for the role. A week later I got a phone call saying that I had been placed in a Guest Relations area. In nine months I had gone from crying hysterically in the DisneyQuest break room to the most desired and prestigious role in the parks.

TWO

You've probably seen me before. Maybe you were waiting in line somewhere on Disney property and happened to see a short little girl standing up ahead of you. Maybe you looked at her and thought, "it's ninety six degrees outside, why is that person wearing what appears to be a wool vest and stockings? Why does she look so tired?" That was me. Maybe you were one of those guests who tapped me on the shoulder and asked, "What are you doing?" I might have given you a glossed-over explanation of a VIP tour and then handed you a business card, because I was not about to tell you my price-per-hour going rate to bypass the Peter Pan line while waiting in the Peter Pan line.

The true role of Guest Relations is a little hard to explain. In short, it encompasses everything. There were some days I sold admission tickets outside the park to guests who barely spoke English. There were other days when I stood at the Tip Board and guests would approach me and ask, "so... where are the rides?" Other days I booked dining reservations and recovered lost and found. One day I stood in Fantasyland for eight hours and told guests that they couldn't enter Fantasyland that day. Some days I was told I needed to run through Frontierland in the rain with a wheelchair to recover a stranded guest.

In short, I used to say: *You know when like it rains, and the parade is canceled, and the guests want to go and yell at someone about that? I'm the person they'd come to yell at.*

The first Guest Relations host was Walt Disney himself. This was back at Disneyland, and Disneyland was Walt's playground. He used to wander around the park and was more than happy to stop to explain anything to anyone; you just had to ask him to. Over time, there became such a demand for information, and knowledge, from Walt that he realized he couldn't do it all by himself. He needed someone else, or a team of Cast Members, to be able to answer all of these questions.

The first Guest Relations hostess was a woman by the name of Cicely. She sold admission tickets from her little ticket booth outside of the park, and Walt noticed that her ticket line was always the longest. He couldn't figure out why it took Cicely so long to sell day admissions. So Walt, being a true investigator, decided to sit in Cicely's ticket booth and watch her sell tickets. Instead of just selling tickets, Cicely planned out detailed itineraries for guests as they entered the park, telling them what to see and do and where to eat. Walt realized he needed a department of Cast Members to handle just general questions and any concerns that might arise. Cicely was Guest Relations Cast Member #1.

Even with Cicely's detailed maps, guests used to get lost in Disneyland. Wanting to avoid chaos, Walt decided to set up actual guided tours of the park, where trained Cast Members would show you around and help you get on some rides. Soon that evolved into an actual memorized spiel that these tour guides would deliver to guests as they walked through the park.

When Disney World opened in the fall of 1971, there was a minimal guided tour available that spanned three-and-a half hours, included about five rides, and cost adults $6.50, not including park admission. Children were $3.75. For 1972, the price of this tour went up 25¢. Anyone could take that basic tour, but if you were an invited guest of the park (or company, or Johnny Depp) you were given a personal guide to get you around everywhere, and when necessary, sneak you in through back doors to ride attractions much quicker than everyone else.

It wasn't really until the 1990s that someone had the brilliant idea to open up a true VIP service to the general public willing to pay with blood and their first born. When I started as a VIP Tour Guide the hourly rate was right around $175 for a basic VIP package (six hour max, limited number of FastPass rides), $275 for the premium (stay as long as you want, ride as many rides). When I left, the basic tour no longer existed and the premium was pushing $355.

I started as a part-time hourly Cast Member at Magic Kingdom Guest Relations. I was being paid about $9.35 per hour. I was guaranteed barely one shift as a part-time Cast Member and most weeks I was given one shift: Friday night, 11pm-5am.

That's a real shift that Cast Members have to work at Disney World. Let that sink in for a second. I was a college graduate with a four-year bachelor of science degree in communications, working six hours a week *overnight* for less than ten dollars an hour. When I got home around 6am the next morning, my roommate was just getting up and leaving for work. I couldn't tell my days apart and I was so tired all of the time. I couldn't pay any of my bills with barely $50 a week. I couldn't afford anything. I was secretly eating my roommate's food when I got up at 1pm. I couldn't afford my own groceries.

After about four months of doing overnight shifts, I interviewed with Disney Special Activities, the branch of Guest Relations in charge of VIP tours. It was referred to as a cross-utilization; I'd still be a guest relations Cast Member, but in conjunction with that I could do these tours. I needed working hours, and I needed the money.

I thought my interview went horribly. They asked me easy questions and I completely fumbled through all of them. I left the interview that afternoon and called my mom crying, saying that I was packing up all of my belongings and moving back home because if I couldn't be a VIP tour guide I was basically a Disney World Cast Member failure and there was no use staying any longer. Instead of driving straight home I drove straight to Menchie's Frozen Yogurt and got myself a $7 tub of frozen yogurt to eat and I ate it all sitting in the driver's seat of my car. That $7 was basically an entire hour of work for me, and thinking about that made me cry, too.

A week later I got a phone call from one of the VIP coordinators, and he informed me that I had been chosen to train as a VIP tour guide.

"REALLY?" I screamed into the phone. I jumped up and down out of sheer excitement, lost my footing, and fell into a metal guardrail. I had a blue bruise on my arm for a week and a half.

THREE

Lets start with the basics. A VIP Tour. That's a tour when guests hire a personal tour guide to lead them all over Disney World, and sometimes beyond. A VIP tour consists of one tour guide, and up to ten guests. As soon as the group hits eleven guests, a second VIP tour guide is required, and the guests will be paying full price for both guides. The tour guide is hired by the hour, with a six-hour minimum. The tour can start at whatever time of day, and can be however long, or short, the guests wants it to be. If the tour is less than six hours, the guests will still be charged for six hours. My shortest tour was just about two hours; my longest was seventeen.

The tour guide is the walking park map, park historian, and designated Fun Captain! for the family. The tour guide takes care of everything so the family doesn't have to; they can just sit back, enjoy their vacation, and watch the tour guide freak out over lost dining reservations at Mama Melrose's. The tour guide has a car, and can pick you up at the hotel and take you right to the park. If the tour guide takes you right to the park, you don't have to wait in long turnstile lines at the entrance! No, the tour guide knows the secret back ways into all of the parks, and will drive you right backstage to a designated gate, where you'll unload and enter the park through there. No turnstiles necessary.

The tour guide is the walking FastPass for all designated FastPass attractions. Do you want to ride Big Thunder Mountain Railroad fifteen times in a row? No problem! You'll breeze in and out through the FastPass line and you can ride to your heart's content. There is no limit to how many attractions you can ride in a day, and the tour guide is the best person to plot a clear path through the park to maximize your fun.

Do you want to ride Pirates of the Caribbean? You can't. See that really long line there? The 40-minute one? The tour guide can't cut that line. That's against the rules. Right now if you go to the Magic Kingdom you *can* in fact cut the line. But back in my day as a tour guide, I couldn't. If the guests wanted to ride Pirates, we had to wait in line. There were a handful of rides across property that we as tour guides just couldn't access. Pirates of the Caribbean, Small World, Tea Cups, Dumbo, Spaceship Earth. Those rides were off limits unless the guests wanted to wait in line. Those were attractions where there wasn't a designated "alternate entrance", so if we were to cut the entire line, *all the other guests waiting in line would see us*. I didn't have the patience to try and cut these lines.

Oh, are we done with Magic Kingdom? Do you want to go to Studios? Lets go hop into my 15-passenger van and drive to Studios! That's what we were allowed to do on a tour. We had complete free roam (within reason) of the Walt Disney World property because honestly no one outside of tours really knew what we could and couldn't do. I had my DSA Blackberry phone on me, and that was it.

As a tour guide, I was in charge of everything. If the guests wanted to eat, I made a dining reservation. If the guests wanted to see a show, I arranged for seating. If they needed something changed at the hotel room, I had to awkwardly call up the hotel and beg the front desk staff to do something for me because if I didn't do it, the guests were just going to go back to the hotel and yell at the front desk staff anyway. I was basically the messenger. Often times I got shot.

I wasn't the only one in charge of the magic on a tour. I was in constant contact with the Office and the tour coordinators there who were the ones making things happen behind the scenes. If I needed to make dining reservations, they were the ones to do that for me. They booked parade viewing, fireworks viewing, transportation arrangements to and from the airport, and they took the credit card payments. The guides were like Tom Hanks in *Apollo 13*; the coordinators were Gary Sinese, now of Mission: SPACE fame. If something went wrong, I called the coordinator for my tour. If the guest's credit card bounced, the coordinator called me and I had to awkwardly ask the guest for a working credit card that could have $3,000 put on it.

This is all just for a regular Joe tour. This is for the family from New York City with money to blow that would hire me for four days at a time to lead them all over the parks and entertain their children. This isn't a "celebrity tour". This wasn't for a PEP tour.

No, those were worse.

But I'm getting ahead of myself. I haven't even told you about Wish Lists. As guides, we were allowed to make a list of up to four people that we'd love to host on tour if they ever came to Disney World. Four people and four people alone, and we had to spell their ACTUAL name correctly, or it got completely messed up in the system. I witnessed one guide throw a hissy fit because he had Pink on his Wish List, but someone else had Alecia Moore. Guess who got to host her?

Most of the time the Office forgot to check the Wish Lists before they assigned tours, leading to a lot of disgruntled tour guides. When I learned I wasn't the guide for someone on my Wish List, I locked myself in a supply closet at Team Disney and cried for ten minutes.

The coordinators made the task of assigning guides to tours sound like they were akin to Walt synching sound to *Steamboat Willie*. Supposedly, there was some fine science to pairing the two parties together, but their methods escaped me. Usually, I felt that they paired tours by playing darts sans dartboard. One time my best friend, Claire, was assigned a tour that only spoke French. She spent the day trying to Google translate words on her phone, gave up, grabbed a park map in French, and told the guests to circle what they wanted to do. I was less than helpful, since I could only remember how to say the words "dinosaur" and "pancake" in French. Sometimes I'd end up with a tour that clearly wasn't suited for me, and I'd wonder what I was being punished for.

A question I was often asked was, "Why did you become a VIP tour guide?"

For this question there is one answer, and one answer alone. If a VIP tour guide tells you differently, they are lying through their teeth. You become a VIP tour guide not for the money, not for the freedom, not to ride rides with football players. No, you become a VIP tour guide for the food.

All the free food you could ever possibly want to eat at Disney World. A million corn dog nuggets at my disposal every single day.

I used my VIP dining card like it was a Deluxe Meal Plan, so yes, I *am* going to have an appetizer, an entrée, two different fountain beverages, and dessert and coffee. As soon as I became a tour guide, my company-issued ID was encoded to allow me to use it as a credit card so I could buy food throughout the park. The tour Office understood that sometimes tour guides would be out for 12+ hours, and might not get a proper break to sit down and have a decent meal. So, they paid for all of our food. Sometimes this was just a banana and a diet coke while my guests rode Speedway, and sometimes it was dinner at Le Cellier if the guests were eating there and invited me along. The largest bill I ever rang up was $99. Christmas Day, Nine Dragons, EPCOT.

One afternoon during tour guide training, we were given etiquette lessons because the coordinators didn't trust us as far as they could throw us. A majority of our tours would be spent with the Joneses and the Smiths, but every now and then we might get a CEO of a company, or an actual foreign dignitary, and we couldn't use our hands to eat French fries. Our trainer tried to instill into our heads that we were to use the "European" way to eat, and not the "American" way, and certainly not "my way", which was usually eating right from the take-out container.

Maybe you're doing some of this math in your head. I've already told you what a tour costs, and I'm telling you how much I would spend on food over the course of the day, so you're probably like, Annie, you are making so much money!

Incorrect.

After a year in Guest Relations I started making $10.63 an hour, the same wage I received for VIP tours. I had pretty good paychecks when I went into overtime. But I was still barely surviving.

What I'm about to tell you will be taboo. Everyone knew it was taboo, everyone still knows it's taboo, and it was a discussion that happened between close friends when no one else was around, and usually behind shut doors. I mean, I was a tour guide, providing a service to guests, and *what happens if they tipped me?*

When I started as a guide, we were not allowed to accept tips from the guests. It was an unacceptable, unapproved practice. If they insisted, we were allowed to take it, but we weren't allowed to keep it. We needed to drop it in a safe back at the Office, and we could either donate the money to charity, or to the mysterious "Guide Fund" that would sometimes put on parties for us and sometimes bought us bagels in the morning.

That's what we were supposed to do. No thank you, no thank you, no thank you, okay this money is going to charity, thanks! It was drilled into our heads again and again during training: *you are not allowed to accept tips. No matter what the guest says, you are not, under any circumstances, allowed to accept a tip.* Disneyland tour guides were allowed to accept tips because the rules for declaring gratuity were different in California than in Florida back in the day. Florida wouldn't allow for that kind of cash transaction. Way to go, Walt.

Thanks for picking the state that won't allow me to take money for riding Star Tours three times in a row. My repressed motion sickness could not withstand multiple rides of that.

It was an unspoken agreement between guides that no one discussed "stickers". That's what we called them. We were living in an abundance of real Mickey stickers, and the term just kind of caught on one holiday season. Stickers happened, like the common afternoon thunderstorm in Florida. That's how tour guides really made their money: a firm handshake that was full of cash.

There were good days for stickers, and then there were bad days for stickers. Sometimes, the guests were so awful I kind of expected stickers to make up for the horrible day they had put me through. Sometimes the family was so awesome, I didn't care if I got stickers or not, because I'd hang out with the Smith family a million more times for free. Sometimes the guests would literally toss a $20 at me, and that was kind of a slap in the face, considering how much they had just paid for the entire 10-hour tour. I once had a guest buy me a ton of groceries in lieu of stickers. That was actually pretty awesome.

The worst was hosting a return tour for another guide, having the guest thank me in stickers, and not knowing what the other guide had done with them. Had they turned the stickers in for the Guide Fund? Did the stickers go to charity? Did the stickers go into the tour guide's vest pocket? I'd stand in the supply closet holding the stickers in my hand trying to figure out what to do while contemplating the price of an oil change for my car. Was the Office keeping close tabs on the sticker flow? It was something that kept me up at night, and every time I was called over to a coordinator's desk I just assumed Mickey knew what I was doing and I was going to need to surrender my ID.

Guests often asked how much commission I was making off the tour, and I'd look at them through sunglasses, completely confused. Guests just assumed my gratuity was included in the exorbitant hourly fee. If that had been the case, I would most definitely own my fair share of DVC property by now. However, it wasn't. Tips weren't allowed, so it wasn't include in the bill.

Now stickers are completely cool for guests to gift to tour guides. Please thank your guide well. Considering how much Disney merchandise they buy each month, they could really use that extra money.

I had freedom to roam the Walt Disney World property with my guests, but there were limits to my magic. I couldn't cut lines;

I couldn't cut anyone in front of us in a FastPass line. This bothered guests a lot, who wanted to know why they were paying *so much money* to stand in line with other guests. What I tried to explain again and again to guests was the fact that, yes, we were waiting with other guests, but as soon as we were done with Rock 'n' Roller Coaster, we could immediately go ride Tower of Terror. All the other guests couldn't. The other guests had to rely on the flawed FastPass system to ride rides, while we just had to rely on me. As long as I was with them we could *ride all the rides*!

At the end of the tour day I had to drive my company supplied vehicle back to the Office, drop it off, file away all my food receipts (my many, *many* food receipts), and do some simple paperwork. Then we were free to clock out, go home, sleep for maybe like three hours, and come back and do it all again tomorrow. The fabulous lifestyle of a VIP tour guide.

Any schmuck could be a tour guide; but it took a really good schmuck to be a good tour guide.

FOUR

Family of three. Mom, Dad, Son, six hours, Magic Kingdom. That's all the information I knew about my first tour. I stared at the tour sheet for a solid five minutes before I decided to print it out and take it with me. I was supposed to meet the family at 9am on the steps of City Hall. It was 8:15am.

The drive from the Office, located across from Downtown Disney in the cruise-like-looking building of Team Disney, to Magic Kingdom took about fifteen minutes. I parked my giant gold Suburban in what I hoped was a designated parking spot backstage at Magic Kingdom. I honestly couldn't tell half of the time. Everyone seemed to have the right of way in this parking lot, and at least half the cars were parked illegally anyway.

I breezed through the gate next to Tony's and made my way across Town Square to the steps of City Hall. The building was full of guests, as usual, and I took up a spot on the front steps to wait for mine. Instantly, I was swarmed with questions about dining reservations and birthday buttons.

"That's inside!" I called happily to them, pointing to the open double doors that would lead to the City Hall counter. "Someone will help you out in there!"

"What are you doing?" asked a boy by the name of Matt, the current Cast Member assigned to work the front porch like a carnival barker.

"It's my first tour," I nervously told him, making sure that none of the guests around us heard. "I'm waiting for my family."

"Oh," Matt replied. He scribbled a name on a birthday button and handed it to the guest. "Are you meeting them here?"

"Yes, 9am, City Hall steps. So if you see them, tell them I'm here." I took a few steps down the stairs and towards the tree located right outside of City Hall. I didn't want to keep answering questions for guests, and I didn't want to get roped into any guest situations. I stood close enough to the building that I was visible, but far enough away to make it clear I wasn't actually working the area today.

9am came and went and no guests showed up to greet me. I pulled out my Blackberry and scrolled through my emails, thinking that maybe I had gotten the meeting location wrong, or they had canceled, or *something*. Nothing. The emails I had were all about park hours for the day, and that fireworks viewing for tonight was full, and that I needed to clean my gold Suburban when I was done with it.

9:15am, still no guests.

By 9:30 I was getting worried. The Office told me that the guests were only going to be paying for six hours, and the clock had already started. But, like, what happens if the guest is mad that we're starting late but still ending right on time? Do I have to tack on another half hour to the tour and not charge them for it? Will I still get paid? Do I have to have someone approve this?

"Annie?" Someone called from in front of me. I turn to face my family of three, Mom, Dad, and Son age 9.

The Dad sticks out his hand. "Sorry we're late. Traffic," he says, pointing back towards the turnstiles. I nod, like I totally understand that traffic is the reason we're late. I awkwardly stick my hand out and shake Mom's hand, and then lean down and shake the boy's, too. "This is Billy." Dad says, as little Billy weakly takes my hand, not sure how to shake it.

"Well, are you guys ready to get started?" I say, my voice cracking in a thousand different places. Thankfully, Magic Kingdom was about six decibels too loud, so they didn't hear my nerves.

"Yeah, what did you have planned first?" Dad asks.

Oh. Yeah. That's right. I'm in charge of this. This is my tour, I am the tour guide, and I'm the one who's going to decide what we do. That's me.

"Uh, well, have you guys, uh, been here before?" I asked as we began our walk down Main Street.

"Last time we were here Billy was 3. We want to hit all the rides for him. I was thinking we could go to Tom Sawyer's Island later and let him blow off some steam."

"There's nothing to do on Tom Sawyer's Island," Mom said, joining the conversation. "It's just an island."

"We'll see what we can do. What do you guys want to do first?" With Billy being 9, their last visit was probably five years ago. I bet I could lead them to literally anything in the park and proclaim, "THIS IS THE BEST THING IN THE PARK."

"You lead the way!" Dad says, grinning.

Main Street is a lot shorter when you're in panic mode.

"How long have you been doing this?" Dad asked me, as we turned at Casey's Corner.

The correct answer would have been, "about forty minutes!" but instead I told Dad, "Three months." It sounded like enough of a time frame where I wasn't completely new, but still new enough to not know everything yet.

I led the family into Adventureland. It takes about five minutes for Billy to start complaining that it's too hot in the park and that he wants something to drink. So we stop and get Billy a drink, and then we continue on, passing Magic Carpets of Aladdin and passing Jungle Cruise.

"What's that?" Dad asks as we walk.

"Jungle Cruise, it's a boat ride." I tell him.

"Lets go do that. Lets ride that, Billy, that looks fun!" Dad was already walking down the slope towards Jungle before I have time to stop him.

Dad's already at the FastPass entrance for Jungle, so I hurry down the slope to catch up to him. I pull out my orange premium DSA pass that said, I CAN RIDE THIS!! and we walk through the queue. We reach the boat. The Skipper asks me how many are riding, and I tell him, "Three!"

"You're not riding?" Mom asks. Mom gives me a look that basically tells me I have to ride. Or else.

Eleven minutes later we're off Jungle and heading towards Pirates. As we get closer I look up at the wait time posted above and it reads "10 minutes".

"Come on, lets go ride Pirates!" I call to the family, as we queue up through the maze of ropes and chains. We walk about halfway through the line when we stop.

"Why are we waiting?" Dad asks.

"Oh, there's only one line right now, so everyone's in this line."

"Why aren't we walking to the front?"

"There are just a few people in front of us."

"Can we cut them?"

"We're almost there!"

We were not almost there. We were still ten minutes away from our boat. Dad was not happy. Mom once again gave me a look that told me I needed to get into the boat with her, and I obliged. We rode Pirates together. Billy hated it. Who knew that the kid hated drops?

Dad really wanted to go to Tom Sawyer's Island. He wanted to let Billy run free for a little bit, hoping that he'd burn off steam and then sleep the entire car ride back to the hotel in Downtown Orlando. I explained to Dad again and again that there was nothing to do on Tom Sawyer's Island except wander around.

Mom fought it, I tried and tried again to talk Dad out of it, but in the end he won. Mom, Dad, Billy, and I got on a raft to Tom Sawyer's Island. Dad was paying through the nose for me and he really wanted to spend an hour watching Billy run around a fake island. This was real life. I gripped the edge of the wooden raft and prayed that no other tour guide would walk along the Rivers of America and see me, pale and frightened, traveling to Tom Sawyer's Island. I wondered what would happen if the raft ran aground and I had to call the Office explaining that I had just saved a raft full of guests from the Liberty Bell.

We got off the raft on the island and immediately Billy took off. Dad found a nice rocking chair just off the dock and settled down in it. Mom followed. They both looked to me, and without any spoken words I knew what they wanted me to do. They were paying through the nose so I could babysit Billy on Tom Sawyer's Island.

I took off sprinting after Billy, in my little blue skirt and black flats, and that boy was fast. I barely caught up to him and chased him all the way to the fort on the island. Once at the fort, he wanted to run up and down the stairs, and I had nothing to do but follow him. I had to follow him. I couldn't very well return to Mom and Dad and explain that Billy had been lost to the island. Wherever Billy went, I went. There are secret passages in the fort that go to other places on the island, and Billy insisted that we go through them. He went into the dark scary crevices first, and I followed. I couldn't see, and my black flats kept slipping on the damp rocks.

Billy then needed to run across the barrel bridge, not once, not even twice, but five times. You know exactly what bridge I'm talking about. The barrel bridge is directly next to the queue for Haunted Mansion. Every time Billy ran across the barrel bridge, I followed him across the barrel bridge. Five times. Five times I went back and forth as the freelance entertainment for the Haunted Mansion queue. At one point some guest in the line clapped for me, and I thought about taking a bow. I hadn't let Billy fall into the Rivers of America, so yes, I should be rewarded Tour Guide of the Week.

An hour later we left the island. As soon as I reached the dock in Frontierland, I swore off Tom Sawyer's Island on a tour, because that was ridiculous. On my first tour, I had already realized that I don't get paid enough to run across a barrel bridge with a nine year old.

The rest of the six hours passed quickly. Billy was tired and didn't want to do anything else, and I was exhausted myself. I led Mom, Dad and Billy back to the same spot where I picked them up. Dad then reached into his pocket and pulled out his wallet. He thumbed through some bills, and I could see he had multiple $20s and at least two $100s. He counted out a few bills, pulled them out, and handed them to me. "Thanks for the tour," he said. Dad shook my hand and disappeared towards the turnstiles.

Time stopped around me. I stood in front of City Hall holding the money, and I slowly looked around to see who had witnessed the transaction. I looked to the steps of City Hall, where I saw Matt, still standing there as if he hadn't been allowed a break since the last time I saw him. He wasn't staring at me; he was staring at the money in my hand. He then made eye contact with me. Time resumed.

"Uh, money from lunch!" I yelled to him, as I shoved the bills into my vest pocket and took off across Town Square without looking back.

I got back to my gold Suburban and climbed into the driver's seat. Once inside, I pulled the money out of my pocket to count it. I have no idea how Dad calculated that tip, but I didn't even care. I didn't know what to do. I was completely paralyzed with the cash in my hand. The little voice inside of my head told me that I needed to turn it all over to the Office, but the other voice inside of my head reminded me that I needed groceries this week. I drove back to the Office, still not sure what I was going to do. Before I got inside I pulled one bill and tucked it into my purse. Gas money, I told myself. The rest of it went to the Dana Farber Cancer Institute in Boston, where my best friend in high school was working as a lab assistant. I hope Dana Farber knows what bridges I had to cross to get them that money.

FIVE

I once made the allusion that being sold for a VIP tour was like the wench being sold by the auctioneer in Pirates, and I was promptly told to never refer to the VIP booking process like that again. Just like the one time I spent an entire day referring to the Magic Kingdom Utilidor (The "underground tunnel", but not really an underground tunnel) as the catacombs. I was once again promptly told to never call it that again.

But honestly, what sounds better?

"Who wants to go into the Magic Kingdom Utilidor?"

Or: "Who wants to go into the Magic Kingdom Catacombs?"

SIX

THE THINGS I CARRIED IN MY TOUR GUIDE BAG

- My personal cellphone.
- A charger for my personal cellphone.
- Wallet with only a credit card in it. Only for emergencies.
- Hairbrush.
- Powder foundation.
- Toothbrush and toothpaste.
- Hand lotion and hand sanitizer.
- Body spray.
- Tiny deodorant (only applicable during summertime).
- Bottle of ibuprofen.
- Vehicle keys.
- 8 fl oz. bottle of water.
- At least two granola bars.
- Tootsie Rolls, Starburst, and LaffyTaffy (but no chocolate; you know what happens when chocolate gets hot).
- Crayons.
- Small notebook for notes, which was really used for autographs that I always forgot to give back to kids.
- Nail file.
- At least two half-eaten granola bars that I forgot were in my bag.
- Keychain flashlight.
- Park maps. Just in case.
- Umbrella. Which never fit. Which I carried. So I'd leave it in the car and then it would rain.
- Extra pair of tights.
- Sunglasses and regular glasses.
- VIP business cards.

SEVEN

Maneuvering guests into queues was a learned skill, not a simple one like learning to ride a bike, but something more difficult like hibachi cooking. One did not just simply put guests into line.

"Where are we going next?" Billy asked, as we walked along through Studios.

"Toy Story. It's like a giant video game. You're gonna play it! And it's in 3D!"

"Cool!" Billy turned to his sister, Sally. "It's like a video game, Sally!"

"Cool!" They said again in unison.

The first thing we needed to do was park the stroller. The stroller parking for Toy Story was located right outside of the exit. The thing about Toy Story is that no one ever anticipated it to be the most popular attraction out of all four of the parks, so no one thought, "Hey, maybe we should anticipate thousands of guests that will want to ride each day, and make a comfortably large stroller parking area and maybe a queue that isn't on top of the sidewalk, what do you guys think?" I wasn't invited to that meeting.

The stroller parking area was nestled literally on top of the walkway between the buildings, and there was never enough space to accommodate the throngs of strollers parked outside. Without fail, no matter where I parked the stroller it was in a different location by the time we exited roughly twenty minutes later. There were Cast Members tasked to organize stroller parking, but they acted more like stroller police.

Sally jumped out of the stroller and went to stand with her brother as Mom and Dad and Grandma and Grandpa and Second Aunt twice removed brought up the rear. "This way!" I yelled, as I held my hand up in the air, gesturing for them to follow me towards the entrance.

The Toy Story entrance was always crowded like a flash sale at the mall. The group of guests directly in front of us was trying to gain access to the FastPass return queue two hours early. The guests standing to the side of us were confused as to why they weren't given FastPasses when they entered the park that morning. The group just behind us was yelling about where they could get the FastPasses to ride.

"All FastPasses have been distributed for the day!" the greeter Cast Member yelled, and then turned his attention to me. "How many?" he asked, bored with his day job and his life.

"I have seven friends."

"Seven including you?"

"Eight including me." Sometimes I forgot I counted as a person through the lines. I pulled my DSA ID hooked to my hip and showed the Cast Member my orange premium pass. He nodded, and counted my guests as we entered.

Down the hallway, past some giant life-like toys, around the corner, and then we stopped at the log cabin. My college program roommate Meg worked at Toy Story, and she always used to talk about the Log Cabin like it was a vacation destination. She just wanted to spend one night sleeping in there, and then make bacon for guests in the queue the next morning. It was hard to not pass the Log Cabin and laugh out loud thinking about that notion. Meg would throw back the curtains as you grabbed your yellow glasses and yell, "WHO'S HUNGRY?" I wish it happened.

The merge Cast Member stood up ahead of us, trying to figure out how many to let through the standby line. I hadn't checked the wait time for it before we got in line, but on a good day Toy Story's wait was right around 75 minutes. On a bad day it was close to 180 minutes. The movie, *Toy Story*, has a running time of 83 minutes. Waiting to ride Toy Story you could watch all of *Toy Story*. I found that to be the easiest day to describe wait times to kids.

"How many?" the girl asked me with distress in her voice. "Seven. Eight including me." She nodded, and let four people from the standby line go. They hurried up the stairs to the bridge like they were just called as contestants on *The Price Is Right*. The girl signaled for me and my group to go, and I hurried after the lucky souls set free from standby.

"Whoa, are we gonna shoot a cannon?" Billy asked, placing his face against the glass overlooking the ride track.

"Yes. You're going to shoot at targets on the screens! And for this ride, everyone needs a riding buddy. So if you don't have a riding buddy, get one." I said this line every time I needed my guests to group off in pairs, and every time I said it no one picked up on the fact that Sheriff Woody tells Andy's toys to get moving buddies.

Mom and Dad paired off with the kids, Grandma and Grandpa were going to sit together, and I was left to sit with Second Aunt twice removed. "I'm actually not going to ride this one," I said to Aunt, who didn't seem too hurt learning she was going to be alone. "I have to make a phone call." Some days all I wanted to do was ride Toy Story because who wouldn't want to be paid to ride Toy Story? Seriously. At first I was hesitant to beat little kids at the game. Then I realized my destiny in life was to continuously receive not only the highest score out of the car, but also out of the hour. If I didn't get the highest score, I forced the family to re-ride for my own hubris. After a while I no longer felt guilty completely creaming the little kids, since they were so impressed I could reach such a high score.

We reached the bottom of the stairs, and the Cast Member at merge asked how many. "Seven!" I said. "Two, two, two, one single." She nodded, and sent us to appropriate rows. Meg always used to complain that smart-aleck guests would tell her numbers like seven and a half, or five and three fourths, and then she'd have a panic attack.

I stood in the corral with Mom and Sally and desperately tried to catch the attention of the Cast Member standing on the other side of the loading dock. I needed to tell him that I wasn't riding, and that I needed to cross to the other side to wait for my guests. I had this huge fear of getting trapped in the loading area of Toy Story, or worse yet, falling into the ride track. I wasn't scared of, you know, being crushed by a Toy Story car, but more the fact that if I fell into the ride track, Toy Story would emergency stop, and everyone in the 80-minute queue would have to be evacuated out and it would be entirely my fault.

The cars pulled up, I darted across the row and turned to wave goodbye to my tour family. They had already forgotten about me, though, and pulled their restraints down and disappeared into the first show room. I needed to make a "phone call", which was actually code for "I really have to go to the bathroom and I'm starving". Toy Story gave me enough time to do both of those things. It wasn't a ride trifecta, though. It wouldn't give me enough time to use the bathroom, get a snack, *and* check the messages on my personal phone.

I raced around the corner, and disappeared through a door that clearly told me CAST MEMBERS ONLY. I had six minutes to accomplish everything I needed to do. I had run down this Toy Story hallway so many times the coordinators no longer questioned what a tour guide was doing using their bathroom. I was in and out quickly, only fighting with my tights for a second, and then I hurried out the adjacent break room door, which led outside. I wiggled past strollers and dads holding maps, and a green army man, and put myself at the back of the popcorn line. I wanted water and lemonade, and maybe a granola bar, and most certainly a chocolate chip cookie. I was able to procure all of those things and shoved the food into my bag as I chugged the lemonade with literally seconds to spare before I needed to get back inside and to the unload area of the dock, waiting for my guests. I somehow managed.

"How was that?" I asked, as they piled out of the cars. I wiped a drop of lemonade off my chin. I had literally chugged it.

"Again!" Billy and Sally cried.

I repeated everything. Again.

EIGHT

I learned very quickly how to be a tour guide; I had to. It was a sink-or-swim situation and some weren't cut out for it. Like it was common to see tour guides and coordinators yelling at each other, it was common to see guides crying hysterically at a coordinator's desk. It was like going off to war if the parade route was our trench. If I hesitated for even a second when answering a question, the guests would sense I didn't actually know the answer. I had to be ready with a response for everything because the guests could smell tour guide fear.

The second they smelled fear, they started asking for things they knew were outlandish and impossible. VIP viewing for Osborne Spectacle of Dancing Lights. Private Safari vehicles. A driving tour of backstage Studios. Fireworks viewing from the top of Tower of Terror. Cogsworth meet & greet. All impossible things, but if I appeared weary on any topic, it was like the guests knew to press the issue more. I needed to be completely resolute with everything I said. Guests would ask questions regarding things I didn't have the slightest idea about, and I'd literally say the first thing that came to mind. Hey, Annie, how thick is the sidewalk we're standing on? It's about six feet. Everything was about six feet to me at Disney.

Guests assumed I could do anything, and everything, for them. In reality I was only in charge of the rides and getting the family to lunch on time. I had no control over anything at Disney, except for the fact that I could re-ride rides again and again. However, guests thought I was like second in command after CEO. They assumed I was invincible and asked outlandish things. No, I was never going to approve a guest feeding a giraffe from a safari vehicle on my watch. I was asked that question at least twice a week. There aren't enough trees in Animal Kingdom to cut down and turn into paper for the liability contract guests would need to sign if I let them feed a giraffe from a moving vehicle. Yet, when I took a second to explain to a guest they were not going to be able to feed a giraffe, they looked at me like I must be joking.

"So what are we paying for?" Dad would then ask.

The guests were paying for the convenience of not having to worry about anything. I was well versed and adept at moving through

Disney World, so with me in the lead they weren't going to have to spend time trying to figure out where to go next, what to eat, where the bathrooms were located, what time Fantasmic! was on that night. That was my job.

For someone who's never been to Disney before, it can be a very overwhelming experience for both kids and adults alike. I witnessed more breakdowns over missed parades than I would ever care to see. You know, I get it. Going to Disney isn't a vacation; it's a quest for fun, like Clark Griswold once said. One morning I was driving to pick up guests and Lindsay Buckingham's "Holiday Road" came on the radio and I thought to myself, *this is as real as it's ever going to get.*

Guests were always impressed when I gave them a brief itinerary of the day, explaining what rides we were going to do before lunch, where we were going to stop for lunch, and then what was after lunch, dinner, fireworks, bedtime. They were so impressed with my ability to manage time and get everything accomplished, and I wanted to break the bad news to them that I was just really *really* lucky with my timing. I could never anticipate when the next showing of PhilharMagic would begin. I guessed. Thankfully, most of the time I guessed right and we got to sit in air-conditioning for fifteen minutes. One time I managed to get into the line to meet the princesses just as they were coming back from ""tea time"" and when my family was let in, the little girl got to meet Cinderella, Aurora, and Snow White all at the same time. Three princesses for the wait of one. The family was flabbergasted that I had arranged such a special meet and greet for them! I thought to myself, "I'm the queen of Disney World!"

I was in charge of the family's vacation while they were with me. Sometimes it was just a six-hour day in Magic Kingdom where we'd race to every attraction as quickly as possible to cram it all in. Sometimes it was a four day vacation and I got to pick where the guests ate every single day. (Boma. Everyone always ate at Boma if I were in charge.) I wasn't questioned too many times about the tour guide choices I was making, though a few times I was strong-armed into taking the family into It's Tough to Be a Bug, even though I advised them that we could spend our time better elsewhere, like maybe cleaning park benches at Saratoga Springs.

All the family members on my tours were the same: Mom and Dad, and kids usually named Billy and Sally. Sometimes I would refer to the parents by Mr. and Mrs., but only when I felt no connection with the family. Usually they just wanted me to call them by their first names. I look ridiculously young for my age, and I didn't want to call Mom and Dad by their first names, so I just called them Mom and Dad, and the kids on the tours always thought that was hilarious. For a few hours each day I had a newly adopted family of a mom and a dad and some younger siblings. If there were multiple moms and dads on a tour, they got numbers, like Mom #1 and Mom #2. Sometimes there were grandparents and aunts and uncles, and I'd call them whatever the kids called them. I acquired a lot of Bubbies doing tours.

I walked through the park thinking, *This is what Beyoncé must feel like when she walks out on stage.* I felt so powerful. I didn't have restrictions like other Cast Members. I wasn't assigned a trashcan to stand next to it all day and remind guests to please avoid the trashcan. I knew everyone was watching me move, both guests and Cast Members. Sometimes it was unnerving. One wrong move and the Office would get a call about me, and I'd get a discussion the next time I went in. I managed to avoid all discussions. The most that was ever discussed with me was, "We need to talk about your corn dog nugget eating habits."

"Here, let me push," I said, trying to edge my way in between Mom and Dad. They were leisurely pushing the stroller through Studios, and we were getting dangerously close to missing our lunch reservation at Sci-Fi. Someone once told me that Sci-Fi is the most popular restaurant on property. I'd like to see Sci-Fi duke it out with Chef Mickeys and see who comes out on top. It was by no means the most popular on property, but it was the restaurant with the most ludicrous seating arrangements. Guests would sit in convertible mock-ups to enjoy their meal, watching a giant film screen before them. A family of four was fine eating at the tables meant for even number parties, a family of five was awkward. Someone either had to sit three to a row, or someone sat awkwardly behind everyone else in a row to themselves. Usually that person was me. I quickly stopped eating at Sci-Fi with my guests.

Due to this cockamamie arrangement, it also took forever to actually be seated. I needed to check the guests in 15 minuets before their reservation time, not 10 minutes after. But they had wanted to sit through Voyage of the Little Mermaid, and who was I to object to that.

But now Mom and Dad were taking their time, strolling past the outdoor merchandise carts, and asking Sally if she wanted a light-up Minnie hat. Of course Sally wanted a light-up Minnie hat. I wanted a light-up Minnie hat. The light-up Minnie hat turned into a Minnie doll, and an autograph book, and a baseball hat for Dad, and we were still nowhere near Sci-Fi.

"I'm fine pushing, you lead the way, Annie!" Dad told me. "Oh, cool, is that American Idol?"

"Yeah, you go check the show times. Let me push!" I said, once again trying to take control of the stroller with Sally. Dad relinquished his grasp, and I grabbed it before Sally had time to roll away.

Dad wandered over to the show times, and I pushed the stroller as quickly as I could in the direction of Sci-Fi. Mom saw me dart away, and she hurried after me. She had to hurry after me. I had Sally and I was pushing her into a crowd, which I had learned was the easiest way to make sure the family kept up with my pace. As long as I had the kids in a crowd, the parents would follow me blindly no matter where I went.

I pushed down the slope towards the ABC Commissary, and Dad saw us disappear around the corner. He left American Idol and followed us. "I can take the stroller back," he said, reaching the bottom of the hill.

"No, I'm fine, I've got it. I have a degree in stroller pushing," I said, like it was a true fact.

Dad laughed. "Then lead on!"

I parked the stroller across from Sci-Fi with literally seconds to go before the family would be deemed "no-shows" for their reservations. "Hey, Sally, can you jump out?" I leaned down to ask her. She mustered the strength and swiveled her legs out. I ran to the podium and checked the family in, apologizing profusely to the seater that we were late for the reservation, and she told me not to worry about it. They were called less than five minutes later.

"Aren't you joining us?" Dad called, as they disappeared down the darkened hallway towards the dining room.

"No, you guys enjoy! I'll be waiting here when you're finished!" I called back, as they turned the corner and disappeared from my sight.

I looked at my watch. It took about an hour-and-a-half to eat at Sci-Fi. Not only were the seats stupid, but service also took a ridiculously long time, like they drove their own fifteen-passenger van to EPCOT to pick fresh greens from The Land. I looked at the ABC Commissary next door. It was time to feast like a king. It was time to eat like I might never see food ever again, or at least until the end of this tour.

NINE

There's this scene in *UP* where Carl and Russell are walking though the jungle, and Russell is complaining about everything. He's yelling that he's tired, and that his knee hurts.

"Which knee?" Carl asks.

"My elbow hurts," Russell whines. "And I have to go to the bathroom!"

"I asked you about that five minutes ago!"

"Well, I didn't have to go then! I don't want to walk anymore. Can we stop?"

"Russell, if you don't hurry up, the tigers will eat you."

Replace the word Carl with Annie, the word Russell with every-single-child-on-a-tour, and the word tigers with Mickey's Jammin' Jungle Parade. That's the quintessential essence of every single VIP tour.

TEN

You never forget your first time driving out onto the tarmac to meet an awaiting plane. Mine happened two weeks into my tour guide tenure.

One of the coordinators printed out a detailed map for me to follow to get to the private airport located way down Route 192 in Kissimmee. I got lost twice and kept turning into the same pawn shop parking lot. Then, finally, down a long and dusty dirt road, I found the tiny little airport. I was early to meet the plane, so I pulled into the parking lot and sat there for about a half hour. The plane was late.

I turned the car off and walked into the tiny terminal. There was one woman standing behind the desk and a technician seated on the couch in the waiting area. Both of them asked me if I wanted anything to eat or drink, and even though I declined I was given water and a bag of popcorn.

"Where's your car?" The technician asked. I pointed outside to the parking lot. "Nah, bring it around, I'll open the gate for you!" The technician was up and moving before I had time to protest.

I got behind the wheel of my Suburban and waited for the metal gate with barb wire lining the top to open. It slowly crept back as I moved my giant car forward. I have only ever seen cars on tarmacs for the president, or in the movies, and usually immediately followed by a Bond villain reveal. It was just a vast empty space, and I didn't know where to go. There were no parking spots on the tarmac. The technician pointed for me to drive a little bit farther, and then park. "You're off the runway!" he yelled with a smile, like that made me feel a whole lot better. I just had this imagine of the plane coming down right on top of me and having to explain to the Office how a small charter plane destroyed my Suburban.

I sat in my car on the tarmac, like this was a normal thing for anyone to do.

I saw it appear in the sky, a little white plane with a blue racing stripe on the side. It slowly began to descend from the sky, which probably happened a lot faster than I thought, but it was still a great distance away from me. It got closer and closer and I heard it now, the loud low rumbling of an engine flying through the sky. It landed on the tarmac with a screech, and I smelled burnt rubber.

The technician went running over to the plane, and waved for me to follow him over. At first I assumed I should get out of the car and walk over, then I thought about how I shouldn't really be walking across the tarmac like that. I drove my Suburban over and parked it next to the plane like something so commonplace I had done it a million times before.

The stairs lowered down. A tall gentleman stood at the top, wearing a blue polo shirt and drinking a beer.

"Do you want some steak?" he called to me. I stuck my head out my window.

"I'm fine, but thank you." I meekly replied back.

"No, you gotta have some steak, the cook's already made it."

I don't eat steak, though. And here was this guy on his own plane telling me that I needed to eat the steak that was already prepared. "Okay." I got out of my car to ascend the steps of the plane, but Dr. No brought the steak to me. He handed me a plate, and an accompanying fork and knife, and told me to eat it while his henchman loaded the car with suitcases.

I ate like three small pieces of the steak, and then politely handed it back to the flight attendant from the plane, who looked at me with such disgrace because I had cast aside a piece of steak probably worth both of our daily salaries combined.

Next on Dr. No's roll call was the pilot of the plane himself, who got out of the plane and handed me his business card. It said his name and then PILOT in big letters. He asked me if I had a business card, and I fumbled around in my tour bag for one of the general cards tour guides were given. I wrote my name on the back of it with TOUR GUIDE in big letters.

Dr. No had two kids, and I wondered if they had ever traveled on an actual commercial airline before. I was told that the trip to Disney World was just a "layover" before their actual destination of the Bahamas. They were stopping for twenty-four hours to see Mickey Mouse like I had stopped on my drive to Orlando at South of the Border to pose with that giant billboard.

Little did I know this was actually a commonplace thing. Guests with their own private airline transportation would literally just pop in and out of Disney World like they were spending the afternoon at grandmas. I'd be told to meet guests in the middle of the afternoon, and I'd need to get them back to their plane before the end of the night. The pilots would just sit in the plane like I'd sit in my Suburban, and spend the time by watching Netflix on their iPhones.

Of course these guests had money to blow; they had hired me. A smart and savvy Disney guest knows how to navigate the park without the use of a $5 a minute tour guide ($300 / 60 minutes = $5. A five minute bathroom break cost $25.). But these guests didn't want to have to worry about learning their way around Disney World, which is where I came into play. I had countless guests tell me over the years that being with me was the first "stress- free" vacation they had ever taken. It *was* stress-free, because I was the one stressed and on edge so they didn't have to be. I had to think about fifteen different things at once, and then account for the fact that Dr. No wanted to see Fantasmic at 8:30pm and the pilot wanted the wheels up at 9pm.

Dr. No and his family were a wonderful tour group, but I watched him throw money every which way and I thought about casually suggesting that he adopt me as an adult child so he could help pay off my student loans, which he could easily do in about fifteen minutes while it would take me fifteen years. Superfluous money dumbfounded me. The fact that Dr. No had his own plane continued to bewilder me. I was eating a steady diet of grilled cheese and eggs to try to save money because I was spending all of it on grande iced coffees at Starbucks. I wondered if Dr. No's kids had ever even had grilled cheese before, or was their life just full of prepared steak on airplanes?

ELEVEN

The biggest lie I ever told a guest was, "Animal Kingdom's closed!"

Sometimes it'd be 4:30pm, and we'd all be standing in Studios, and I could tell that the family was winding down, but then the hyper fifteen-year-old boy would yell out loud, "Yo, Mom, can we ride Everest again?" Mom would look to me for approval of this plan, and I had one of two options:

Take them to Animal Kingdom at 4:30pm, knowing that there was no way I could get in and out of there in less than an hour, and as soon as we made it into the park they were going to want to ride Safari, again, and probably see Festival of the Lion King for its last performance of the day at 5:30, so we wouldn't leave the park till after 6, get them home just before 7, back to the Office for just before 8, out of there before 9, home for 9:30pm. Asleep fifteen minutes later. Pass.

Or I could tell them, "Oh gosh, Animal Kingdom closes in a half hour. The animals have to go to bed!" No one was ever going to argue with the animal's bedtime. Animal Kingdom's closing time was always shaky to begin with, because it did closer earlier than the other parks, and were guests really keeping track of that time? Sometimes they'd ask, "Can we see the fireworks at Animal Kingdom?" A serious question, with a serious answer of, "The animals don't like fireworks." Just like how the animals don't like straws or balloons or lids on cups. I spilled so many diet cokes for the sake of the animals.

TWELVE

Fountain View Ice Cream (as of late, a Starbucks) always smelled like waffle cones. I would stare longingly at the ice cream location as I trudged with guests from one side of Future World to the other. I always desperately wanted to stop, because they not only had waffle cones, but they had waffle bowls for ice cream, and they'd also make ice cream cookie sandwiches. It'd be a thousand degrees, and I'd be racing guests from Soarin' to Test Track, and vice versa, and I'd only think of ice cream. There was no scenario where I could stop in and get myself a scoop, though. My guests needed to want the ice cream, too, and they never wanted to stop to get a hot fudge sundae. No, we needed to be in and out of EPCOT in about an hour and a half so we could make our dinner reservations back at the hotel. There was no way I could position them in front of the fountain so I could be, like, here watch this fountain show for fifteen minutes while I go wait in this line to get myself a snack! I couldn't step away and get a snack. The guests needed to want the snack for me to get one, too.

Sometimes I'd casually suggest it. Like, hey guys, it's really hot, how about we stop for a refreshing treat? And the guests would always be, like, but Annie we wanted to ride Test Track twice before dinner. Take us to Test Track, Annie. We want to ride in a yellow car.

My plan for ice cream always fell through.

Billy tugged on my sleeve. "Annie, can I have ice cream?"

"Can *I* have ice cream?" I asked Billy, as we walked from Future World West to Future World East, Billy keeping up with my pace as I pushed Sally in the stroller in front of me.

"Yeah, we all can have ice cream!" Billy happily cried. Sally cheered from her seated position.

"Billy, I'm not in charge of the ice cream." I told him, as we passed by Fountain View and I longed for some mint chocolate chip.

"But I want ice cream!"

"So do I, but your parents are the ones who make that decision. I'm not in charge of the ice cream."

"Then what are you in charge of?" Billy asked, looking at Fountain View himself. He struck me as a kid who would enjoy chocolate chip or cookie dough ice cream.

"I'm in charge of the rides, Billy," I sighed, as I pushed the stroller.

"Huh?" Billy didn't get it.

"Like the Lorax speaks for the trees, I speak for the rides."

"Who's Lorax?" Great, I had Billy the kid who had never read a Dr. Seuss book in his life.

"Like, I make the decisions about the rides, for the rides," I tried to explain. "I'm like the delegate from rides. The ride delegate."

"What's a delegate?"

"Like in government…" I started, and then I looked over at seven-year-old Billy and I realized he didn't have the slightest idea what I was talking about. The kid just wanted some ice cream. "Never mind. Maybe you can have ice cream with dinner."

THIRTEEN

Here's a stupid word for a really simple thing, *porte-cochère*. What in the blazes is that, Annie? It's a covered driveway. It's that location where you drive up to the hotel to drop off your bags and your kids and the valet guys come running forward to open doors and take your belongings. I kept on hearing this term again and again during training, but I didn't want to be *that kid* who asked for a proper definition. I let this word slide for weeks and weeks and people kept on telling me I needed to go to the *porte-cochère* to get guests, and I'd show up and say, well, they were waiting at the valet stand for me, so...

I just never put two and two together. Every time I tried to Google the word I spelled it horribly wrong because it's French. Finally I asked one of the valet guys, and he looked confused and then he had to go and ask someone else and finally it got back to the Grand Floridian duty manager who laughed at me. He explained it was just the valet area. It was the covered area so guests could unload their luggage in a rainstorm without getting wet. It suddenly made so much sense.

During training, we were told that we should arrive at least fifteen minutes early to the *porte-cochère*, or, as it will henceforth be known as, the valet. For my first week of tours, I arrived to the valet fifteen minutes early. Then I quickly learned that guests are notoriously fifteen minutes late, if not more. As much as I'd love to stand outside and await the hordes of guests who will ask me questions just before they get on a bus for the parks, I'd much rather spend those extra few moments at the Office getting Starbucks coffee from the coffee cart.

It didn't matter that I didn't fit in with the Disney theming of the Grand Floridian; I was wearing a nametag and looked important holding car keys and a Blackberry in my hand, and everyone honed to me like guests to Dole Whip. Most of the time the questions were like, Where is the character breakfast? Where is the bathroom? Where is the bus? What time did the park open? What time are the parks open until? Can you bring my car around for me? I slowly started noticing that the guests would come to me for every question, leaving the actual hotel greeters with nothing to do. So they'd socialize. So the later I showed up, the more it gave the actual hotel staff something to do.

To become a tour guide, I had to pass a driving test. It was nothing like the driving test I took to get my license. This test involved driving an obstacle course backstage at Animal Kingdom in a 15-passenger van. It was the same driving course they used for bus drivers, so obviously that'll translate well to tour guides. I showed up to take my driving test a week before my tour guide interview, and I was wearing shorts and a green sweatshirt hoodie. I jumped behind the wheel of the 15-passenger van and I drove the course twice. I had to accelerate correctly, I had to maneuver around cones, I had to back the van into a parking spot without turning my head around ("What happens if there are guests blocking your view out the window?"), and I had to do so without hitting any cones ("What happens if you're backing in next to Phil Holmes' [vice-president of the Magic Kingdom] car?"). I have no idea how I passed my driving test, but I did.

The test did not fully prepare me to actually drive the 15-passenger vans every day. They were literally like driving a small mini bus. I took ridiculously wide turns, I was constantly adjusting my mirrors, and I felt every single bump I went over. The vans were noisy and smelled funny. But, they fit fifteen people, so they were necessary.

If I wasn't driving a 15-passenger van, I was driving a Suburban. Spoiler alert: the Suburbans became the bane of my existence. I found them to be worse than the vans. The Suburbans were like driving a mini bus on steroids. They had a million blind spots, but they also had heated seats. I couldn't get a car seat into the third row, but I got satellite radio. I felt powerful driving a black Suburban around Disney property, but I also hated having to pull into and out of every single parking spot. In 1971, the Imagineers did not design parking spaces suitable for a Suburban.

Thankfully, though, mini vans were eventually added to the fleet of VIP vehicles, and every chance I got I begged to drive a mini van. The mini vans were roughly the same size of my own little car, plus they also had satellite radio, plus it comfortably fit everyone in for soccer practice.

Driving a Disney company vehicle was intimidating. I mean, my mom didn't even let me drive her own car, and here was Mickey handing me the keys to Lightning McQueen. Every morning after I arrived at the Office I had to find my vehicle assignment, grab my keys, and then check to make sure that the vehicle was in good condition for my guests. Sometimes it was clear that a popcorn fight had happened in the backseat of a car; sometimes it was clear that every single person in the tour had gone through the Bibbity Bobbity Boutique since glitter was sprinkled everywhere.

At the end of the tour I had to fill the car's tank up with gas, and conveniently the Disney gas pumps were in the scariest locations on property. My favorite gas pump was located right behind Magic Kingdom, but that was so far away from everything. The closest gas pump was at Caribbean Beach, waaaaaaay in the back of the complex and tucked behind the hotel's service center. This location also appeared to be the graveyard for discarded items from Pop Century, and as I would fill up a mangled looking 5-foot Mr. Potato head watched me suspiciously.

I'd drive around property, a little tour guide in a giant car, and on nice Florida days I'd roll the windows down and turn up Radio Disney as loud as possible and sing along to whatever One Direction song happened to be playing. I listened to a lot of oldies, too. Sometimes if I was late to meet guests it was because I was listening to "What A Feeling" from *Flashdance* in my 15-passneger van.

One day I bought myself two chocolate chip cookies (from Sunshine Seasons) and I only ate one of them; I put the other one in the center console of my van. The tour was long and difficult and it was ridiculously hot in the park, and when I dropped the family off at the end of the night all I wanted to do was lie down and sleep. I climb into my van and started unloading my belongings and popped open the center counsel only to remember that Past Annie had left Future Annie a chocolate chip cookie, and it was the best thing I could have ever done for myself. I started constantly buying multiple cookies and hiding one of them in my van for the end of the tour. There was nothing like finishing off a long tour with a Sunshine Seasons chocolate chip cookie.

FOURTEEN

98% of all my tours started at Disney deluxe hotels, and 95% of those tours started at the Grand Floridian. Next year for Christmas the Grand Floridian should ask Santa for a bigger valet.

For being the most popular and desirable resort on property, the valet was a tiny little thing. The hotel opened in the summer of 1988, and way back then I guess the Imagineers never thought that someday there might be fifteen tour guides with fifteen gold Suburbans waiting to pick up guests at 9am. We'd all stand together like the motliest gaggle you had ever seen, all with our Blackberries in hand, furiously checking updated park information. We were psyching ourselves up for the day.

It was 8:57am one morning, and I was just pulling up to the Grand Floridian security booth. Even the security guards recognized me after a while. I flashed my ID badge at them, and the security guard told me to have a "magic day" as I drove forward and towards the valet. It was already crowded for so early in the morning. There were two Magic Express buses and three tour guide cars, and what felt like three dozen other cars belonging to guests who were somewhere in the process of checking in and checking out of the hotel.

I pulled underneath the monorail station. The valet manager signaled me forward, and then signaled me to back into a spot next to the white carriage outside the Grand Floridian entrance. I shook my head "no".

He shook his head "yes".

I shook my head "no" again and pointed farther down the valet, towards the actual parking. The valet manager shook his head "no". He held up his finger to signify "one second" and attended to the car ahead of me first. Once they had pulled away he came to my driver's side. I rolled down the window.

"Can you back into that spot for me?" he said, pointing towards the white carriage again. I could see that there were three other suburbans already parked over there, and all of them had been backed into their spots.

"Do *you* want to back into that spot for me?" I asked him.

"It's not that hard, I'll help," he offered, but I kept shaking my head.

"How about I jump out and you can do whatever you want with this car?"

"You're scared? What, did you hit something?" the manager asked. I looked at his nametag. It said TREVOR.

I made a face. I actually had hit something once. I got horribly lost at Old Key West on one of my first VIP tours, and wedged myself into a really tight space by accident. I'm a short little tour guide, so no, I couldn't see out all of my blind spots in the suburban. The car had a reverse sensor, but it couldn't tell when things were to the direct side of the back bumper. I was backing up, backing up, and as soon as the back sensor registered that I was about to hit something, it was too late. CRUNCH. I jumped out of my Suburban to discover that I had completely shattered a taillight against a pole in an Old Key West parking lot. The best part is that my tour family watched it happen, and then made fun of my driving for the next four days. The only damage done was the broken taillight, but the Office reacted like I had hit Pluto.

I told Trevor this story. He laughed. "Here, let me." He opened my door and I jumped out. He climbed in, readjusted the seat ("It's like you're driving on top of the wheel.") and seamlessly backed the Suburban into a tiny space next to the white carriage.

Trevor tossed my keys back to me. "Let me know if you're going to need help pulling out, too," he said with a chuckle. He was very tall and lanky with short brown hair curled over the top of his forehead. He had wire frame glasses and wore black slacks with a purple shirt and a skinny gray tie. If I were a Disney Princess, and he a Disney Prince, that's where our love story would start: the Grand Floridian valet.

Considering I spent most days waiting at the Grand Floridian valet, I learned Trevor's schedule. I knew that if it was Wednesday, and I was picking up my guests at 10am, I wouldn't see him. But if I were dropping my guests off around 8pm, he would be there. He'd see me drive up and he'd wave, and I'd wave, and then he'd gesture for me just to park wherever I wanted because he was just going to move my vehicle anyway. It was a really nice relationship. He'd ask me about my tours, and I'd ask him about what it was like moving cars. Whenever I'd leave the Grand Floridian he'd wave goodbye, and observant mothers on tours would ask, "Is there something going on between you two?"

Yes, because he moves my car for me so I don't have to. There's a lot going on right there.

FIFTEEN

Sometimes, the hardest thing for me to explain to a guest was that the Pirates of the Caribbean ride came before the *Pirates of the Caribbean* movie.

"That's so cool, they made a ride about the movie!" Little Billy excitedly cried as he rushed towards the Adventureland building. I should have just let it go. I should have just let Little Billy assume that this ride had been built in 2003 and not four years after the park opened.

"Actually," I started, as we made our way into the winding queue line. "The ride came first."

"No way!" Billy said with wide eyes.

"Yes way. This attraction has been here since 1975."

"That's so old! How did they know the movie was going to be so popular?"

"No, Billy, the ride was here first. In 1975. And then the first movie came out in 2003."

Billy tried to do this math in his head, though math wasn't needed for this explanation. "So, the movie is actually, like, really old?"

"No, the movie came out in 2003. Captain Jack was added in 2006."

"So, they made the movie and the ride at the same time? Did they make the movie here?"

I should have just said, yes, Billy, they shot *Pirates of the Caribbean* inside Pirates of the Caribbean. Synergy. "No, Billy. The ride was built here way before the movie. Then, Disney decided to make a movie based off of the ride."

"Did Walt Disney direct the movie?" Yes, Walt's last project was not *Mary Poppins*, but instead *Curse of the Black Pearl*.

"No, Walt passed away in 1966. Before the ride. Before the movie."

"That's so cool that they made a movie about one of the pirates inside!"

"No, Billy. Listen to me. The ride came first. Then they made the movie. And then the movie was so popular they put Captain Jack inside of the ride. It's a ride that inspired a movie that inspired the ride."

"Wait, this ride's been here the whole time?" Billy's dad piped in.

No, oh my gosh, was I going to have to Wikipedia this for the guests? "The ride was built here in 1975. Then a movie was made based off of the idea of pirates in the Caribbean. And then, with their success, figures from the movie were placed inside the attraction to tie it all together."

"Cool. So did they do any of the filming here?"

Yes. *Pirates of the Caribbean* was shot on location at Pirates of the Caribbean in Adventureland, Disney World, Orlando, Florida, USA. Tell your friends.

Actually, don't. The Pirates Cast Members already have enough trouble reminding guest not to take flash pictures and to keep their hands out of the water; I don't want them to have to snuff any other situations.

SIXTEEN

After three months of being a tour guide, I started telling guests that I had been doing it for six months. That seemed reasonable. I wasn't new anymore, but I was still very much figuring out my footing.

"We requested a seasoned guide," Mrs. Grey said to me as I drove the 15-passenger van down World Drive towards Magic Kingdom. "I hardly think you're qualified to be doing the tour."

There aren't enough superlatives in my vocabulary to fully capture how awful the Greys were to me. I was their fifth guide; they had already destroyed four other guides before me. When I first learned of the tour I was pulled aside by one of the coordinators and told in a hushed voice, "They're pretty mean, so just don't let anything get to you."

When one of their former guides heard that I was hosting them, he asked, "Why are you being punished?" It was just one of those cases where I was the only guide available, and sometimes sacrifices need to be made. I was prepped on the fact that they were going to be rude, ungrateful, loud, obnoxious, and complain about literally everything.

I met them at the Waldorf valet promptly at 9am, but they would later claim I was a half hour late and thus impacted their day in the park. They were the motliest crew I had ever met. To put it nicely, Mrs. Grey was overweight and Mr. Grey looked like he was still a teenager. One of the other guides had told me that it was an arranged marriage for the two of them, and it made complete sense. They had one daughter, age four, who refused to acknowledge my presence. She spent most of the day crying to the nanny who wouldn't buy her anything in the park. Along with the four of them were an uncle and an aunt and their two kids. There was also another adult male in the group, who I assumed was another uncle, but turned out to be Mr. Grey's Lover. He informed me he was Mr. Grey's "mister" and I didn't really have anything to say back to that other than nodding my head like I completely understood when really I wondered why he felt the need to divulge that information to me.

I spent six hours with the Greys. These are the some of the things that went wrong:

THE FAMILY BELITTLED ME FROM THE GET-GO.

We weren't even in the park yet. We were standing in Park 1 when Mrs. Grey informed me that she didn't feel our VIP tour service was that "VIP". She went on to explain that she had been to other theme parks in the area, and found their tour services *much* more desirable. These other parks treated their guests like real royalty, and would literally cut every single line and jump right to the front to expedite all wait times. I tried to explain to Mrs. Grey why other parks can get away with doing that, but she cut me right off to inform me that, "We're only using you for the transportation to and from the park."

Oh. Okay.

Mrs. Grey then explained that she had one of our "assistant passes", the now-retired GAC (Guest Assistant Card), for guests with disabilities, that would help her navigate the lines without me, anyway. Mrs. Grey then told me she had cancer. *We still weren't even in the park yet.*

THE FAMILY REFUSED TO GET OFF SOME OF THE RIDES.

Knowing their daughter's age, I decided that "small world" would be the first attraction. It didn't have a FastPass, and if we were going to ride it, it needed to happen as early in the day as possible. We arrived at the park just after 9:30am, before there were too many other guests trying to fight their way onto "small world".

It took us a half-hour to walk from where we had parked the car to "small world". It took us this long because we had three strollers for three different kids, and every kid wanted to go in a different direction and buy something else. They must have dropped over $100 before we even made it to Fantasyland. And by the time we reached "small world" there was already a fifteen-minute wait. It didn't look like it would be that long, and I didn't even mention to the guests that it might take a few extra seconds. I ushered them into line. We managed to get through the queue in less than five minutes.

I rode "small world" with them because I always like to ride the first ride of the day with the guests, whatever that may be. That sets up for them that I'm a fun tour guide, and I don't mind riding rides if I have to. I foolishly rode "small world" with the Greys.

By the time we got all the way around "small world", the queue line was a little bit backed up. I was sitting in the last row of the boat, behind the family, and Mrs. Grey from the front row turned to look at me.

"Can we ride again?" she asked.

"Yeah, we'll just jump right out of the boat and get back into line..."

Mrs. Grey cut me off. "I'm not getting out of the boat."

I was so taken aback by the comment I opened my mouth to speak but nothing came out. My mouth moved, but I formed no actual words. It took me a solid five seconds to formulate dialogue. "We can't ride again without exiting. The line isn't that long, we'll just jump right out and get back..."

"You are going to make a woman *dying of cancer* get out of this boat and *wait in line again*?" Mrs. Grey roared. She was a large woman and her voice bellowed through the open atrium. We were close enough to the unload dock that the Cast Members loading the boats turned to look at us. The guests waiting in line to get into the next boat looked at us. The guests who had just exited the ride looked at us. The only thing that could have made this moment better was if the boat started sinking.

"Unfortunately, Mrs. Grey, we have to exit out of this boat to get into another boat..."

"I am not leaving this boat."

"...they've already loaded this boat for the next ride and I don't want to hinder other guests."

"I don't care about the other guests. If I want to ride "small world" again, I am going to ride it again."

Our boat reached the loading dock. The unload Cast Member looked at me with such pity and sadness in her eyes I thought I might cry. I stood up to exit.

"Anne, sit down. We are riding again," Mrs. Grey barked at me. I got out of the boat. Every single person in the "small world" vicinity was looking at me. I believe time stopped for a second in Fantasyland. I stood on the unload side of the dock and looked down at my guests. Mrs. Grey clenched her jaw.

"Unfortunately, we cannot experience the attraction again. We are all going to have to exit." But no one in the boat moved. Maybe some of them wanted to move, but they were terrified of Mrs. Grey. I was scared that she was going to start yelling at me, and her words would not be "small world" appropriate. The load Cast Member on the other side of the dock sensed that this situation was not going to have a happy ending and launched the boat with the Grey Family still sitting inside. Off they went once again on the happiest cruise that ever sailed.

I, meanwhile, called the Office to explain that Mrs. Grey had literally commandeered a "small world" boat.

Mrs. Grey pulled this stunt two or three more times before she realized that I actually wasn't going to stand for her behavior. And neither were some of the Cast Members at other attractions. At Winnie the Pooh they refused to send the honey pots around again, and made it clear to everyone waiting in line what the hold up was. I didn't ride another ride with them again all day.

THEY REFUSED TO WAIT IN LINE LONGER THAN A SPLIT SECOND.

We'd approach an attraction. I'd maneuver myself into the FastPass return line, gesturing for them to follow me. Mr. Grey would take one look at the queue, and if he thought it was "too long" he would shake his head and no family members would join me in line. The family literally needed to be able to walk all the way through the queue to be appeased. Guess what never happens in Disney World? That. There is no such thing as a "walk on" attraction, even if you can walk right through the entire line. There's always going to be a stop somewhere, whether it be to count heads as to who's riding in what car, or simply just a slow loading vehicle. There were six guests in line before us for Peter Pan, and Mr. Grey told me that was too long. The pirate ships take off literally every five seconds. We were going to wait for fifteen seconds for a pirate ship, but the family couldn't manage that.

THEY INFORMED ME THAT THEY DIDN'T WANT TO PAY FOR ME TO EAT THAT DAY.

That's cool, Grey Family, you actually don't have to pay for me to eat anything all day. Mickey covers all of my meals since I don't get a true "lunch break" at any point during my shift, so I can cover all of my own meals and snacks, don't worry about it...

Mr. Grey turned to me. He had pulled on his pastel cardigan and looked like a JCrew ad from Connecticut. "Doll, could you cancel our lunch reservations?" Lunch was supposed to be at Tony's Town Square.

"No problem, would you like me to reschedule it somewhere else?"

Mr. Grey turned to Mrs. Grey, and Mrs. Grey shook her head. "I find park food to be disgusting." Oh, good, tell me how you really feel about this place.

I was still trying to make the best out of this awful situation. "Do you mean you just don't want quick service? I know other good locations for table service food, how about Liberty Tree..."

"We don't want to waste time eating somewhere," Mr. Grey said, exchanging a look with Mrs. Grey, who nodded in agreement.

"Lunch will only be forty five minutes."

"We don't want to take the time to eat lunch while we pay you to sit around and do nothing." Mrs. Grey reminded me of Ursula. They were roughly the same size. "It's just poor service for you to charge us to eat *our* own lunch, while you get to go and have a forty-five minute lunch break yourself."

This was the first and only time that topic ever came up. Yes, there were certainly other times guests moaned and groaned about being charged to sit down and eat a meal (there was no pause on the tour guide clock) so I always made sure to reassure them that lunch would be fast. God bless Liberty Tree's soul; they could have guests in and out of there in less than 35 minutes. No real time was ever lost. I always factored in a 45-minute lunch break into my daily planning. Sometimes I did have guests who told me that they didn't want to stop and have a full meal, but they were more than willing to snack all day. So we weren't going to sit in air conditioning for a little bit, but we were going to stop and get popcorn and ice cream and maybe a pretzel. That's all I really needed, too. I just needed something to eat to keep me going.

This was different. The Greys had just told me that they didn't value me enough as a person to let me eat. No one tells me I can't eat. I spent the next few hours stopping Every Single Chance I got to eat something. They were constantly coming off of rides and I was eating something else. It's not my fault they decided to ride the Speedway and I got myself an ice cream sundae and a frozen mocha Frappuccino and a soft pretzel in the shape of Mickey.

THE FAMILY MOVED SO SLOW, AND COMPLAINED ABOUT IT THE ENTIRE TREK, LIKE GENERAL WASHINGTON'S TROOPS WHEN HE TOLD THEM THERE WERE NO MORE SHOES AVALIABLE AND THEY HAD TO CROSS THE ORIGINAL 13 COLONIES BAREFOOT, WHILE I WAS LITERALLY ASKING

THE FAMILY TO WALK FROM ONE SIDE OF LIBERTY SQUARE TO THE OTHER.

I walk abnormally fast. I understand that. Mrs. Grey did not move fast. I moved fast, she moved slowly. I'm more than willing to slow down my pace to keep up with any guest, but she took this whole issue to the next level. I'd be walking and walking and I'd turn to check on the guests and they'd be nowhere in sight. I was wearing a BRIGHT RED PLAID VEST HOW CAN YOU LOSE ME IN A CROWD. I'd retrace my steps fifteen yards and find the guests all standing there, huddled together like a pack of wild roaming buffalo that had gotten turned round at the last rest stop. I'd wave to them in a friendly way, showing which direction I was heading and which direction we should all travel in, and all of them, as if on queue, would scoff at me. How dare I walk faster than any of them? How dare I try and maximize our day. *How dare I.* In the email follow-up that Mrs. Grey sent to the tour Office regarding my "poor behavior" during this tour, that was the first thing she highlighted. How I kept "wandering into crowds, leaving everyone else behind". I wasn't even trying to do it on purpose. Probably subconsciously it was just happening.

THE THREAD COUNTS ON THE SHEETS AT THE DELUXE HOTELS WEREN'T HIGH ENOUGH.

Walking across the Liberty Square Bridge, I overhead this exchange:
   "We checked into the Animal Kingdom Lodge, but checked out four hours later. We tried to take an afternoon nap, but the sheets were so uncomfortable. Called down to the front desk, told me they were only three hundred count sheets. Three hundred count? Considering we're paying three hundred dollars an hour for this tour, I feel like the resorts can get better sheets. We checked out that afternoon, didn't even spend a night there, and came over to the Waldorf ."
   Part of me wanted to tell the guests I had bought my sheets at Ikea on sale and then have everyone guess what count they might be. 100? 50?

THEY INSULTED WALT DISNEY.

Walt loved progress. He loved adding new things to the park, making it better, evolving it with the changing times. He called this process "plussing". Walt once said that, "Disneyland would never be complete as long as there is imagination left in the world." He loved the idea of moving forward and constant change, which he represented in Carousel of Progress, one of his favorite attractions. It's a perfect thing for children and adults to do if they don't want to go ride Space Mountain.

Only two people in the group wanted to ride Space. The Uncle Grey and one of the kids. I offered to take them, and suggested that everyone else go ride the PeopleMover. Mrs. Grey informed me that she did not want to ride PeopleMover, and asked about Carousel of Progress. I told her it was an Audio-Animatronics stage show and would roughly coincide with us riding Space. She seemed to like the idea of sitting down inside for a bit, so I pointed her in the direction of the area to load and I took Uncle and Kid on Space.

We returned about twenty minutes later.

The rest of the family was just exiting Carousel of Progress; they saw us and slowly started making their way over. Aunt asked Kid if he liked Space, and he replied that it was "fine". I turned to Mrs. Grey and asked her what she thought of Carousel of Progress.

We were standing right in between the Buzz Lightyear merchandise cart, and the strollers, and the entrance to Buzz. There were a lot of people around us, since it had turned out to be a pretty busy day in the Magic Kingdom. Standing there, in clear view of other guests, and at full volume, Mrs. Grey turned up her nose at me and scoffed. The next sentence she said to me will forever be ingrained in my memory.

"There aren't enough words in the English language to explain how horrid that show was to sit through."

Sometimes I don't really think before I speak. I've kind of trained myself to do so while on a tour, because the last thing I want is a guest with more money than God calling to complain about me. But I didn't care about this family. I didn't care if they had a good day, I didn't care if their children got to hug Mickey, I didn't care if they got through all of the rides they wanted to do and if they would ever come back to Disney World ever again. I was done with this family and I wanted off of this tour.

So, no, I didn't think before I opened my mouth and replied to Mrs. Grey. It all just happened so fast.

"Well, ma'am, I don't think Walt Disney would have liked you either.

It's time for the parade." I turned on my heels and didn't even bother to check if the rest of the family was following me. I marched from Tomorrowland, down Main Street, and towards the Fire Station where parade viewing had been booked for the family. Strangely enough, they kept up with my pace and we all arrived at the parade viewing location without speaking another word to each other. I checked them in with the Cast Member in charge of VIP viewing, and when they all gathered, penned in between the white parade ropes, I told them, "There's a bus at the TTC that can take you back to the Waldorf. Enjoy the parade!"

I turned and I marched back across Town Square, out the Tony's Gate and I was sitting in my empty 15-passenger van five minutes later.

A few days later I was pulled aside by one of the coordinators who wanted to read me an amusing email. Mrs. Grey had taken it upon herself to write a scathing review of my tour service, in which she called me "inexperienced" and "unprofessional". The coordinator thought it was hilarious. I had come back to the Office after walking away from that family and debriefed anyone who would listen about how awful they had been. Every tour guide has that one awful family that makes them cringe even years later. I can only hope that the Grey Family never puts another tour guide through the strife they put me through in those five hours and forty five minutes. I didn't even last six hours.

SEVENTEEN

Prior to arriving at Disney World, I disliked kids. Kids weren't my thing. I could barely tolerate anyone a year or so younger than me, so stick me in a room with five years olds and I was begging for help. Maybe it was just the fact that I never had a whole lot of interaction with kids. I had younger sisters, but one was only two years younger, and by the time that the youngest one was growing up I was already moving out of the house. I just saw kids as slimy and sticky and probably covered in germs like all those tissue commercials show.

After I arrived at Disney, I learned that kids are the best. Maybe it was just the setting I was meeting these kids in, but I realized that kids were way better than their parents. Their parents never wanted to talk about princesses and *The Incredibles* with me, but the kids did. As a kid going to Disney, I was never allowed to dress up in an awesome costume. Partly it was due to the fact that we were always going in August and it was hot and sticky and my mom never wanted to put me in a polyester costume and run around the park (funny, now I was getting paid to wear polyester and run around the park); partly it was because the costumes were so expensive and my mom thought she was going to pay all that money and I was just going to want to change out of it. So, as a child in Disney World I was deprived of dressing like my favorite princess. I envied the little girls who got to run down Main Street dressed as Belle because I never got to, and I said that to these little girls every chance I could. I also complimented their shoes, and their hair, and their fingernail polish, and told them to say hi to Belle for me because we were good friends. (True. I had a lot of friends who were Friends with Belle.).

With boys I'd be like, "Who's your favorite character??" and the boys would yell back, "BATMAN!" and I'd be like, "Yes, that is correct!" because I was not about to explain to any seven year old that Batman is owned by D.C. Comics and not by Marvel Comics, which is owned by Disney. I always had a soft spot for kids who told me that their favorite Disney character was someone other than a Disney character.

Sometimes the parents were cool and I'd want to hang out with them, but more often than not dads wanted to talk about stocks and golf and moms wanted to talk about gardening and *Real Housewives*. I just wanted to talk about things like "Shake It Up" and Taylor Swift. Coming to Disney made me realize that kids are actually awesome because we liked all of the same things.

I gauged how much I came to like any kid by whether I could remember their name a week later. Guests would often ask who I had hosted the day before, and sometimes I'd stand in a queue and rack my memory because I couldn't remember if I had had boys or girls the day before.

My favorite kid ever was named Jake. He was British. I remember him as British Jake. I met British Jake one spring day in the Magic Kingdom. He was an only child who had his parents and his grandparents with him. The parents were awesome, and the grandparents were awesome and I loved everything that little British Jake had to tell me because he told it to me in a little British accent. British Jake loved pirates and pizza so I made sure to find both of those things for him during our day together. British Jake was also a pretty shy kid, and his parents were amazed he took to me so quickly. We walked through the park hand in hand because that was the true sign of being a good tour guide; British Jake liked me enough to want to hold my hand. At one point during the day I made a joke to Dad about how I was going to be the newest Disney princess in the park.

"When can we buy your merchandise?" Dad asked me.

"It's only available online right now. I'm huge in Tokyo." I told him. For the rest of the day Dad only called me Princess Annie, and the rest of the family caught on. At the end of the tour British Jake asked to have my autograph, and I signed his autograph book "PRINCESS ANNIE OF THE MAGIC KINGDOM". I knew I had completely won over a child when they asked me to sign their autograph book.

British Jake, in turn, gave me a thank you card with Donald Duck on it. I went home that evening and I hung the card on my refrigerator so I could look at it always.

Close to a year passed. It was a ridiculously hot day and I was doing a chaotic tour in Hollywood Studios for a family that didn't really know what they wanted to do so I kept throwing them into shows all day. They were watching Indiana Jones and I was standing in line at Studio Catering Company, waiting for my cheeseburger. I was thinking to myself, *Why is this line so long and will the Office notice if I order two cupcakes just to eat the frosting off of both of them*? From behind me I heard, "I think that's Princess Annie."

I turned to see a vaguely familiar dad with a British accent. I looked down at the child standing next to him and I immediately recognized British Jake. I was so startled that they remembered me, and they were so startled that I recognized them.

"Jake! You gave me a Donald thank-you card!" I told the shy little kid who hid behind his dad for a second. Then he slowly remembered that I was one of his good friends at Disney World, and he came over and gave me a big hug. The moment was short-lived because they had just received their food, and I was next up to order mine. Mom and Grandma waved goodbye to me as they led Jake away. "I'll never forget you!" I called after him. He waved goodbye.

Dad lingered with me for a second longer. "He's going to be shell-shocked for the rest of the day that you knew his name," he told me, giving me a hug was well. "On our screensaver at home your picture always comes up, and Jake will ask when he gets to come visit you again."

I have no idea how I held back tears of happiness standing in Studio Catering Company, but I managed somehow. Dad apologized for not hiring a tour this time, but they were spending most days lounging by the pool at their DVC hotel. It didn't matter to me, though. Not like I was seeing any money from the cost of my service, anyway. I was just happy to see British Jake.

I saw him once more that day as he was loading onto an attraction and I was loading off. I called goodbye to him and he to me, and British Jake and I went our separate ways.

EIGHTEEN

Last time I rode Splash Mountain I was nine years old and the only reason I rode it was because Michelle Tanner on *Full House* had ridden it and I wanted to be just like her. (Why don't TV shows go to Disney anymore?)

I don't like drops and I don't like heights so why would I subject myself to an attraction based solely on those two things. Last time I rode it, age seven, I sat with my dad in the last row, and as soon as we hit the beehives I started crying hysterically, begging him to let me off. Well, you can't just get off Splash Mountain on the final hill. The guy sitting in front of us was taping the whole ride, too, so wherever you are, I'm sorry that you have a hysterical little girl screaming in the background of your home movie.

I'd approach Splash Mountain with my guests and I'd inform them that I couldn't actually ride, because the Office forbids it. "I can't get my costume wet!" I'd tell them, pointing to my wool vest and polyester skirt. It wasn't true, but it was the only excuse I had not to ride. All I needed was one little kid to beg me to ride with them, and I'd have to cave in, and then they'd always remember their Disney VIP tour because they were paired with the guide who cried hysterically on Splash Mountain.

"How about I hold all of your bags?" I asked the family as we gathered into line.

"That'd be so sweet of you!" Mom said, unhinging her Coach fannypack from around her waist. She slung it over my neck and shoulder like a sling. A little bit farther down the line, the two teenage girls draped their Longchamp bags over my other shoulder. Just before we reached the boats, the brother took his backpack off and slipped it around my arms. As the family turned to get into the boat, Dad handed me the three blue merchandise bags they had been lugging through the park with sweatshirts and plush toys and Mom's new Mickey teapot that she just had to buy. They climbed into their log while I fought my way to the overpass stairs like a pack-mule fighting through a herd of cattle. I went up the stairs, across the waterway, and down the other side. One Cast Member at unload told me that it looked like I was "going camping" and I laughed because I was still in earshot of all guests.

The exit route of Splash twisted and turned around corners, and at one point there's a hallway with two doors. The door on the right led nowhere useful for me. The door to the left led into the Splash maintenance bay, and I pushed through that door, waddled down some steps and came out behind the mountain. Splash wasn't the ride trifecta, because I could go to the bathroom and I could check my phone, but there was nothing I could eat within range. Sometimes there was an ice cream cart by Woody and Jessie's meet and greet, but that was only on really hot summer days. There would be no ice cream today.

I was looking for a wheelchair because that's what I wanted to sit on for thirteen minutes while I waited for my guests. I found one in a corner, but it was missing one wheel. I wanted to sit. I was willing to take that chance.

I slowly unloaded my guests belongings, and placed them carefully down onto the ground literally shedding pounds left and right. I checked my phone and calculated ten minutes from now. That's when I'd head back inside to claim them.

I dug through my tour bag, rummaged past the granola bars and the body spray and the small bottle of Advil and the Tootsie Rolls, and found my iPhone buried at the bottom. I pulled it out, connected to the weak Disney wi-fi reception available on the backside of Splash, and checked my emails, my Facebook, my Twitter, my emails again, and scrolled through Instagram. Checked Twitter one more time.

From around the corner of the building, two Cast Members approached, both clad in Splash garb. One held a thick three-ring binger in his hands; the other had an EARNING MY EARS tag pinned to her shirt. They were deep in conversation about the evacuation procedures of Splash Mountain.

"...the yellow lines on the ground will indicate to guests where to go in the event that we need to get everyone out," the trainer was saying. He looked up from his notebook as soon as they had stopped in front of me.

"Hi." I offered, from my seat in the broken wheelchair.

"And this is where the tour guides hide," he said to his trainee. I nodded, because it was true. "Just please don't...fall into the maintenance water with all of that? It's her first day." The trainer gestured to my hodgepodge of belongings, and then pointed to the girl.

"I wouldn't dream of it," I told him. "Well, you know, carry on."

The trainee looked terrified at the notion of anything falling into the maintenance water. I wondered what day of training it was for her, and if she would survive to the end. She looked young enough to be a College Program Cast Member. The trainer led her down towards the maintenance bay, and she stuck close to the cement wall, away from the water, in case she were to trip and fall into the shallow pool there.

After seven or so minutes, I rose back up to my feet and slowly slung the bags and purses and backpacks around my arms and shoulders, and struggled to move forward under the weight. I waddled down into the mountain again, and emerged out the same door I had exited through. I turned the corner to stand in one of the windows of the exiting queue, and dropped the bags to the ground again.

The family exited off the ride a few minutes later, and came rushing around the corner towards me. A few of them were wetter than the others, and I could easily figure out who had sat in the front seat.

"Can we go again?" asked one of the teenage girls.

"If you guys want to," I said, looking to the parents for confirmation that this was okay.

"That's fine, we've still got time till lunch, right?"

"Right. So let's exit out this way..." I initiated movement for the group, as they slowly grabbed their bags from my arms and followed me out of the exit.

Fifteen minutes later I found myself once again sitting behind Splash, in the same wheelchair as before, scrolling through my phone and no one had posted anything new to Twitter. The trainer exited out of the door in the side of the building.

"Have you been sitting here this whole time?" he asked.

"Did you push your trainee into the Rivers of America?"

"It's lunch time."

"Ah. I promise I went through the queue again. And then came back here. Again. Don't tell anyone you saw me back here."

"This is your hiding spot. I get it. Just fold up the wheelchair when you're done?" I nodded and the trainer disappeared towards the Splash break room.

When the family rode a third time, I retreated back to my special spot to find that the trainer had swapped out the broken wheelchair for a new one with working wheels. It was sweet. Or he just didn't want me accidentally rolling into the waterway.

NINETEEN

There were a few words I feared more than anything else on a tour. They weren't, "Billy fell into the Seven Seas Lagoon!" and they weren't, "Little Sally fell off of Everest!" and they weren't, "Grandpa's gone!"

They were, "Our last guide…" and then the family would tell me exactly what their last tour guide had done for them, something I was clearly refusing to do for them now. The most common one was, "Our last guide didn't make us wait in line."

No, the last guide probably *did* make you wait in line, but you're with me now, your new tour guide, and you can't talk me into *not* making you wait in any line. Literally every time I PEPed Soarin' I needed to call someone to ask how to do it, so I wasn't about to spend an entire day calling all of my tour guide friends trying to figure out how I could get this family to not wait in line for anything.

Sometimes tours would complain that I wasn't doing things their prior guide had done, like set up special meet and greets with characters, and arrange for private dining rooms at restaurants, and I'd always bewilderedly respond, "I can do stuff like that?" No one told me I couldn't demand my family ride on the Princess Float in the parade, but I wasn't about to see if I could do that either.

Over time I grew a thick skin and questions like these didn't faze me anymore. No, I'm not going to cut the line at Everest for you, no I'm not going to demand that we get our own private room with Mickey, no, I'm not going to see if I can get the Voices of Liberty to serenade us while we eat in Italy, though it seemed like some guides were more than able to do that. I was not. I wasn't getting paid enough to try and negotiate with the Voices of Liberty.

I received information that I was going to be hosting a return tour for another guide. This guide was going away on vacation, and wouldn't be around when his tour family came to town. I was the only guide available, and I headed out to meet this family early one morning. I had been told that there would be nine in the party, and I drove my 15-passenger van to meet them.

I waited at the Polynesian for maybe ten minutes before the family strolled down to meet me. Dad introduced himself, and we made polite conversation about Disney World and the weather, and I mentally counted how many family members were mulling around. I counted eleven. Dad must have seen me silently count; he quickly informed me that he would not actually be joining the tour. I was going to take his wife, and her sister, and all of their kids off to EPCOT while Dad and Uncle went off to go drink around the world. He gave me instructions to have Mom or Aunt call him when we were done for the day, so they could all meet up for dinner.

I surveyed the kids in the group and mentally planned to take my time wandering around Future World, with the possibility of talking them into a sit-down lunch somewhere like China or Morocco. I needed to make six hours last.

I drove the family to Epcot. Mom, Aunt, seven kids.

When we arrived at Epcot I asked the family if I could swipe their tickets into the park, since park entry was required for every single tour. I was surprised to learn that Aunt's family hadn't purchased tickets for this vacation. I needed to kill time, and these guests needed to purchase tickets. I led the family from the backstage entrance next to Test Track over to Guest Relations right next to Spaceship Earth.

We arrived at Guest Relations and the line was already out the door. I could have easily headed inside, bypassed the line and gotten a Guest Relations Cast Member working the lobby to get me tickets quickly. I could have easily just called the Office and asked them to purchase tickets for me with the guests' credit card on file. For some reason, though, I didn't do any of those things.

Aunt spent a half hour waiting in line. Mom and the kids kept themselves occupied while I stared off into the distance, thinking about what I was going to eat for lunch that day and if I had enough gas in my car to get me home that night. Every now and then another guest would approach me and ask me a simple question about EPCOT. I answered with ease because I knew everything about EPCOT, that's why I was a tour guide. I pointed guests towards bathrooms, merchandise shops, coffee carts, and Minnie Mouse. Mom hardly seemed to notice that I wasn't doting on her and her family; they were fine doing their own thing. I knew they were talking, but I had no idea what they were saying. Did I mention that their native language was Spanish? They mostly spoke Spanish. I still spoke no Spanish no matter how loud someone yelled HABLO ESPANOL? I knew a few phrases, like, "This ticket is only for one park, one day!" and "The bathrooms are over there!" and "Here!" I've never had an ear for languages. I took five years of French in high school, but I remember maybe twenty minutes of it.

I went and I bought myself lemonade and I leaned against the outside of EPCOT Guest Relations and let time pass. Somewhere in the midst of all of this, I realized that Mom was talking to someone. I looked at the Guest Relations line and saw that Aunt was currently at the counter, purchasing her tickets. I shrugged it off because guests were always making friends with other guests. Nothing about the situation was strange.

Finally, Aunt emerged from Guest Relations, waving tickets around in the air and our day in the park was finally ready to start. Aunt corralled her children, Mom corralled hers, and then Mom turned to her new friend, who corralled her children, and everyone started following me into EPCOT. I did a quick head count. Nine people... plus these four new friends. Thirteen people.

Mom saw me do a headcount.

"This is my other sister and her two kids. Is it okay if they come with us?" Mom asked as we stopped in front of the Fountain of Nations (didn't know it had a name, did you?).

I looked at the thirteen people in tow. "I actually can't host any more than ten guests at any time. If you want to add more to the tour, I'm going to need to call the Office and get a second guide."

A VIP tour is often like trying to herd cats. And it's not like herding cats in the wilderness; this is herding cats in Future World. That's why the Office sets a limit of ten guests per tour guide.

"Oh, it's still only ten guests. We're not going to ride anything." Mom pointed at herself, and Aunt, and New Aunt.

"But I can't host more than ten guests."

"But we're not going to ride anything," Mom said again, as if I hadn't heard her the first time over the roaring fountain.

"Three of you have to leave." I told them, standing my ground. Mom turned to conference with Aunt and New Aunt. She turned back to me five seconds later.

"Can you watch the children for us?"

I wish someone had taken a picture of my face at that exact moment in time. It was a mix of sheer confusion, and shock, and I half expected a hidden camera crew to jump out of the bushes and yell, "You just got Disney Punk'd!" I must have looked so dumbfounded. This was the first time parents were willing to, actually trying to, give me their kids. A complete stranger. I know Disney had me vetted before I started as not just a Cast Member but also as a tour guide, but this notion was ludicrous.

I needed to say something to Mom, so I said, "I'm not a babysitter. I'm a tour guide."

That statement offended all three of the mothers *a lot*. They began talking to each other in Spanish so fast I could barely make out any of the few Spanish words I knew. They started walking farther into EPCOT, but I just stood there, planted to my spot on the ground. I wasn't about to follow this madcap family any farther.

"Are you coming with us?" Mom turned and barked at me with her Spanish accent dripping off of her English words.

"I can only take ten guests on a tour, unless you want me to call my Office and get a second guide. If you don't want a second guide, then three people need to leave," I told Mom, not budging from my spot.

This was not the answer that Mom wanted. She looked to Aunt, and New Aunt, said some hurried things in Spanish. "We'll keep the tour at ten. The first ride is Test Track?"

New Aunt wandered off into EPCOT away from us, but I still had her kids with me. So we had dwindled from thirteen... to twelve. I informed Mom of this as soon as we reached Test Track.

"We're not going to ride," Mom said as we stood outside the attraction. She pointed to all of the children, "Ten."

I had twelve guests with me, and only ten of them were going to ride. But that's not how a VIP tour functions. This isn't a rotational free-for-all. This isn't like a buffet where you can pick and chose what you want and then go back for more afterwards. No, I needed ten guests and ten guests alone. I didn't care that Mom and Aunt were going to sit and wait for us outside. All I needed was for one tour guide to come wandering by and count my guests and see that I had two more than I should have and I was going to be in so much trouble.

"For this one attraction that's fine. I'll take the ten guests on, but when I come out we are going to decide who is coming with me for the rest of the day, and the others will have to leave."

"I'll call my husband and see what he wants to do."

I took the kids inside of the ride, all ten of them, while Mom and Aunt waited outside. I put the kids on the attraction and then darted out an unmarked Cast Member door to e-mail the Office.

Hey. It's Annie. Heads up, I've got the Blue Family with me, and they've got 13 people. Don't want to get rid of any. I'm going to try and sort this out, but I might need a second guide.

The Office emailed me back before they got off the attraction. They had a guide on deck if I needed one.

I collected the children off of Test Track and took them back outside to Mom and Aunt who were waiting in the midst of stroller parking.

"I talked to the Office. They have a second guide available if you want to add others to the tour. Did you talk to your husband?"

"Do I get the second guide at half price?" Mom asked.

Do I get my own float in the parade? "No. If you don't want a second guide I need to know who's coming with me for the rest of the day."

Mom looked to Aunt. Spanish Spanish Spanish. Mom told me in English that Aunt was going to leave. So we started walking and as soon as we passed Mouse Gears, Aunt disappeared inside. So twelve guests, to eleven. Still one too many.

"There are still eleven guests with me. I can only have ten."

"Our last guide let us take more than ten guests."

There it is. That's the kicker. Their last guide had let them take more than ten guests and they just expected me to do the same. Mom then began yelling at me, in half Spanish, and in half English, about how this was never a problem for their last guide, so why was it a problem for me? I asked Mom point-blankly if she had talked to Dad about adding a second guide on the tour, and Mom told me she hadn't. Mom pointed to one random child and said that they would no longer be coming with us, and shooed the poor child away from our group. I can only hope that he went off to meet up with Aunt, wherever she had wandered off to in EPCOT. "What's the next ride?" Mom barked at me.

I led the guests to the other side of Future World towards Soarin'. We stopped for a bathroom break before we got into line. It was incredibly crowded, and I stood off to the side, casually leaning against a wall, waiting for them all to exit. When I gathered the group together after the bathroom I once again counted thirteen of them. I don't know how the others managed to finagle their way back to us without me noticing them, but it happened.

"I can only take ten guests on the attraction with me." Mom looked at me like I had just pushed her in front of a Living with the Land boat. Her eyes were fiery red.

She yelled some incoherent things at me in Spanish, and once again tried to give me all ten children. I was not about to play this game all day. I informed Mom that I was going to need an adult to accompany me through the attraction, since I would opt out of riding. So, one child was going to have to be traded for an adult. This sent Mom over the edge. More yelling in Spanish Spanish Spanish. I have no idea how I managed to get ten guests into the queue, but I did. No one spoke the entire queue. I didn't even bother asking for them to be placed in B1. I left them as soon as we passed through merge, darted out another unmarked door, and called the Office.

I decided the best thing to do right now was throw that other tour guide under the bus.

"Their last guide took a group larger than ten. I keep telling them that I refuse to take more than ten, but they won't listen to me and Mom's getting mad. What should I do?"

There have been a few situations where the Office has been less than helpful. This was one of them. They didn't have a good idea, or suggestion, or input, or anything, as to what I should do. They were more than ready to send another guide out and start charging for two guides. I asked them what they wanted me to do. No one seemed able to get in touch with Dad, wherever he was on Disney property, and no one wanted to tell me to end the tour, either. I was alone in The Land.

Mom and the nine kids got off of the ride and she immediately asked where we were going next. Something came over me. (It might have been the adult breakfast bounty I had just eaten at Sunshine Seasons because I had close to 25 minutes before they got off Soarin'. Soarin' takes so long to ride. Each show is 8 minutes long. Every time you don't get loaded into a show, you wait another 8 minutes for the next one. That's an additional 8 minutes that I have to eat something from the deliciously home-grown Sunshine Seasons, the best quick service in Epcot, not counting when Canada lets me take Canadian cheddar cheese bacon soup to go.) I told Mom that she was going to make a decision right now as to who would be my ten guests for the day, and who would leave. That is, unless she wanted another guide who was standing by at the ready.

Mom asked for the next attraction again. I told her that she had until Spaceship Earth to figure out her tour lineup.

We walked in silence. I led my parade of thirteen guests from The Land to Spaceship Earth and no one said anything to each other. We approached the entrance to the best slow-moving history lesson and I turned to Mom for her answer: who was leaving the tour, or would she be getting a second guide?

I know when most guests walk into EPCOT they just breeze right underneath Spaceship Earth and don't spend any time actually lingering by the giant ball. For one, that area is a complete wind tunnel. There's no use in trying to fix your hair or hold a park map if you're passing underneath it. The area is also really open, so sometimes things echo against the metal buildings and the giant metal golf ball. It's also in such a prime location that everyone in that general vicinity is almost completely aware of everything else happening around them. Guests are taking PhotoPass pictures, renting strollers, asking for directions.

I've been yelled at before in my life. Mostly by my own mom, and that usually happened in the comfort of my own home. It never happened to me in front of Spaceship Earth. It had never happened to me in front of so many people, and Cast Members, and so loudly, in Spanish.

Mom screamed at me. Her loud words echoed off the buildings and everyone, guest and Cast Member alike, stopped to see what was happening. They just assumed someone was being torn limb by limb at the entrance to the attraction sponsored by Seimens. It was also all in Spanish. Mom might have been yelling at the top of her lungs for me to take the brunt of the beating, but I hadn't the slightest idea what she was screaming.

Cast Members from both sides of the entrance slowly shuffled out of their location to make sure nothing was going terribly wrong. They found me, a tiny little tour guide, getting destroyed by an irate guest. One boy from the camera shop held his hand up to his ear, making a phone gesture, clearly asking if he wanted me to call security. I shook my head so gently that Mom didn't see others were trying to communicate SOS to me. I think most of the Cast Members who watched this situation unfold were doing so only for the story they could tell their roommates later. "Yo, dude, saw this crazy stuff happen at Spaceship today…"

Somewhere in between Mom coming up for breaths of air, I started to get words in edge wise. When that didn't even work, I realized I didn't even actually care about the situation unfurling in front of me. There was a long pause at one point where Mom reached into her purse for her phone, obviously to call her husband, who had been a brick through all of this, that I told Mom what had been brewing inside of me from the start.

"Unfortunately, due to these circumstances, I won't be able to continue on with this tour. I hope you and your family have a magical day here at EPCOT." And I just turned and I walked away from them.

Mom immediately shut up. I don't think she expected me to turn on my heels and go. She stopped yelling. Returned back to English.

"Where are you going?" she yelled after me.

"The tour is over. Enjoy your day!" I waved to them as I continued to walk farther and farther away. I was walking quite fast; probably because I was worried Mom was going to sic one of the kids on me and drag me back to them.

The entire ordeal spanned two hours.

TWENTY

I was standing in line for Big Thunder Mountain, like I often did, when I felt at tap on my shoulder. I turned around, ready to answer a question for a nearby guest.

"Are you new?" the guest asked me.

"No," I told her, not sure if I should be confident in my answer, or confused.

"Then you should know better than to wear your costume out in the park." She said sternly, and pointed right at my nametag. "You could at least have the decency to remove that. Are you on your lunch break?"

"No?" I told her, now actually confused. The guest stood on the other side of the wooden partition in the line, close enough that we could talk, but not far enough away so other guests around us couldn't hear our conversation.

"Then what are you doing?" she asked, disdain dripping out of her voice.

"Riding Thunder Mountain?" Seriously, what did it look like I was doing?

"Can I have your last name so I can report you to your manager?" she asked. The guests standing around watched us like a tennis match, their heads snapping back and forth with each comment we made to one another.

"Are you a Cast Member?" I stammered.

"Yes, and I'm not stupid enough to go into the park in full costume."

"Are *you* new?" I asked her.

"I've been with the company for six months now," she said, proudly, like she had just been told she was next in line for the VP of Magic Kingdom spot.

"Cool," I said, deeming the conversation over, and turned to follow my guests down towards the loading area.

"You can be terminated for wearing your costume onstage!" She yelled after me, and her portion of the line moved, too, as she crept closer to me. "This is atrocious behavior."

My guests realized I was having a heated conversation with

someone in the line. Billy leaned into me. "Why is that crazy girl yelling at you?"

"I don't think she's ever seen a tour guide before," I told him.

The Disney Narc came up behind me again. "Are you just going to pretend you're in the right?"

"I'm also going to ride Thunder Mountain," I told her, as we moved closer towards the awaiting train. "Is that okay with you?"

Her eyes were fiery red. She turned to one of the Thunder Mountain Cast Members and yelled, "Don't let this girl ride!"

The Thunder Mountain Cast Member looked at me, and I looked back at him, and we both recognized each other from all the times I had ridden Thunder Mountain before, and his name was Jonathan, and I said, "Jonathan, I want to ride in the back." And Jonathan said, "Okay."

I climbed into the car with Billy next to me, and we both waved to the crazy Cast Member standing on the dock, who pulled out her phone and took a picture of me as I rode away into the Frontierland sunset.

TWENTY-ONE

There's this mythical time in Disney lore that's referred to as "capacity". Guests often asked if the park was at "capacity" on a rainy spring day, and I'd laugh out loud at their notion, thinking, there are barely 30K people in the park right now. How on earth do you believe this to be capacity? I'd explain that this was not as crowded as the park could get, and they'd ask me questions like we were sitting around a campfire making nice hot s'mores. They wanted to know about this time called "capacity". I'd tell them capacity was a time when the wait for Space Mountain would be four hours and the wait for quick-service food would be an hour an a half. I'd reference the pathway between Fantasyland and Liberty Square, and explain that sometimes the park would be so crowded that this area came to a complete standstill. I talked about it as if it were the worst battle of Magic Kingdom I had ever fought.

The family wanted to go to Magic Kingdom on Christmas Eve even though I begged and pleaded with them to change their mind. It was a family of four, Mom, Dad, two adorable kids, and the chain-smoking Jewish-grandmother Nancy. She was a sassy broad, constantly forgetting how to operate her EVC, constantly parking it in the wrong spot, getting lost, forgetting the key, asking, "Where's the nearest place to smoke?" We wanted to take the EVC away from her, but we had gotten it for her so she would stop wandering into crowds to smoke. At least on the ECV she was a little bit easier to find.

By the time we reached the park on Christmas morning, all the EVCs were rented for the day. Dad didn't understand how the EVCs could be gone like that, and I tried to explain that there wasn't a secret hidden stash of the motorized scooters. I suggested we rent a wheelchair instead. Dad looked worried with this suggestion and I quickly offered, "I'm more than happy to push."

"Are you sure?"

"Yeah." I wanted to push the wheelchair. Just like the stroller, if I had Grandma Nancy in my clutch, there was a high possibility the family wouldn't lose me in a crowd all day. Or maybe they would. Grandma Nancy was feisty.

I want to describe other things as being as crowded as Magic Kingdom on Christmas Eve. Like, a boy band concert. "There were so many screaming kids there, it was like Magic Kingdom on Christmas Eve!" You will never really know what it feels like to be in a closed-to-capacity space until you've braved Magic Kingdom on a closed-to-capacity day. The park hit capacity at 10am that morning. Do you realize how many people are in the park when that happens? It's astounding; I don't even want to say. If everyone in the park gave me a nickel, I could probably have bought Toontown.

Dad put the two kids in a double-stroller, and we literally used it like a cattle prod to make our way through the crowds. They didn't want to stay all day, but we were staying to see the parade at 3pm so we at least needed to make it till then. We had lunch at a tiny table barely built for all six of us at The Plaza. After lunch the son wanted to go ride Splash Mountain.

Now, this tour was actually pretty cool. They were one of my favorite families, actually. Mom and Dad were wonderful people, and had wonderfully well-behaved children who said "please" and "thank you" and never stuck their hands into the water at Pirates of the Caribbean. I would gladly march into battle for this family, and that's basically what I was going to do, lead them from The Plaza to Splash Mountain.

Dad asked me if it was a good idea to go to Splash Mountain, and I laughed: "Not really," I told him. "But it'll be fun!"

It was not fun. Walking from The Plaza to Splash Mountain should take about ten minutes. It took us close to forty-five. We tried to walk through Adventureland, but that was the worst idea I had ever had, because Adventureland is cramped and crowded no matter what time of the year it is. We cut into Liberty Square, which had a little bit more room to breathe, but not by much. Guests were already lining the way to watch the parade. The viewing area was already five or six guests deep.

I led them onto the river walk, since that seemed to be the easiest place to maneuver. We passed the smoking location.

"Leave me here! Leave me here!" Grandma Nancy cried. I look to Dad for confirmation.

"We'll probably be an hour."

"Leave me here, I'll be fine." Grandma Nancy already had her long cigarette out. She was smoking the same thing Audrey Hepburn did in *Breakfast at Tiffany's*.

"She'll make friends. Maybe one of them will push her away." Dad said to me as we moved away from Grandma Nancy. We had willingly left a comrade behind.

We fought our way past strollers and international tour groups to get to Splash Mountain. I took the family's bags as they jumped into their log and rode away. I darted out the maintenance door for Splash, and collapsed onto the ground. There wasn't a wheelchair in sight, but I was going to sit no matter what.

Thirteen minutes of quiet passed, and then I had to go retrieve the family. They were a little bit wet, but they were happy and the kids asked to ride again and before I could shut that down, Dad suggested that maybe we head off to our parade viewing and get a snack along the way. Deal.

The family stopped to look at their ride photo before we turned into the merchandise shop at the exit of Splash. We had to rope around a few poles, and a candy display, and we had just about made it out of the tiny little store when I felt a tap on my shoulder. I turned around to see a disgruntled guest standing there. I knew she was disgruntled because she was a middle-aged woman wearing a tiara and had a pink fannypack around her waist and was clutching the arm of a small child.

"Are you in charge?" she asked.

"Of what?" I asked.

"I need to talk to someone in charge," the woman said. She smacked her lips.

"Regarding what? Was it something about Splash Mountain? Did you lose a hat on the attraction?"

"I need to talk to someone about this crowd. This is horrible. No one told me it was going to be this crowded today. Where can I go for a refund?" This was one of those guests who believed that it was *my* fault I hadn't personally called her the day before and warned her about traveling to Magic Kingdom on the third busiest day of the year.

Thinking back on situations like this, I wish I had replied to guests with exactly what they wanted to hear. I should have said, "Yes, I am in charge of this today. Who would you like me to ask to leave?"

"Unfortunately, we don't do ticket refunds," I told her instead. If I could keep this guest from storming down to City Hall to argue with Cast Members there, I was going to try. "It's a vacation time so a lot of guests are experiencing the park right now…"

"I don't need to hear that." She snapped at me. "I need to know what you're going to do to fix this."

I realized I didn't see my family in sight. They must have kept walking even when I stopped to talk to this charming woman. "I can't do anything to fix this, it's a crowded day." I told the woman, moving a step away from her. What did she want me to do anyway? I didn't have the time to go around to each and every single guest and ask him or her to politely vacate the park.

"Don't walk away from me!" the woman barked. "Are you not going to do anything about this? Get me your manager."

"Ma'am, you can't yell at me here. I don't work in Splashdown Gifts. Excuse me." I smiled and turned away from her.

"I'm going to tell all my friends about this piss-poor customer service!" She yelled after me, but I had already gotten far enough through the crowd to lose her.

My family was waiting for me outside by the bathroom. They had taken the opportunity to use them, and I was thankful they hadn't wandered away on me. "Everything aright?" Dad asked.

"Sorry about that, guys. I'm clearly in charge of park attendance today, so someone stopped to argue with me about that." Mom threw her arm around my shoulder and told me I was doing a great job. She was a cool mom, I really liked her. The family bought me groceries at the conclusion of the tour. We put our battle armor back on and fought our way back to chain-smoking Grandma Nancy.

TWENTY-TWO

You're probably wondering how many famous people I met while at Disney. I hate to disappoint you, but I didn't meet that many.

For some reason I was always assigned sports figures. Part of me thinks it was because the Office knew I hadn't the slightest idea about anything regarding sports. If they were to put me with a television personality, I never would have let them out of my sight. But instead I was given a slew of baseball players and I'd ask them, how do you like playing for the Bruins?

You probably know this football player, but his name's not important. When I was first told of his name I asked, "Who?"

The coordinator told me.

"And who is he?"

They told me.

"And what sport does he play?"

They told me that.

"I don't know him."

They told me a current event about him.

I Googled him and I was like *oh [insert explicit not suitable for Disney Parks]*.

This sports player, let's call him Bob, was staying at one of the off-property hotels and wanted an afternoon tour. I was the only tour guide hanging around the Office, so by default I got the tour. When some of the guys in Office heard who I was going out with, they begged to take the tour instead of me. I begged for them to take the tour instead of me. The coordinator wouldn't budge: Bob was mine.

I was instructed to meet him at the valet at 1pm.

By 1:30pm I still hadn't seen Bob, so I called the Office to double check that I was still meeting him. The Office reassured me that Bob would show up. 2pm rolled around. Still no Bob. I was bombarded with so many questions I finally told the front desk to call me when Bob finally came down, because I was going to go sit in my car.

Bob showed up just before 3pm.

I don't follow sports at all. You can tell me all you want about sports and I won't understand in the least bit. I will cheer for whatever team you want me to cheer for. Go team. Score the points. I saw Bob exit out of the lobby and scan the valet area for his tour guide.

"You our girl?" he asked.

"Hi, I'm Annie." I said, sticking my hand out to shake his. For a second, I thought he wasn't going to bother shaking my hand. Reluctantly, he did.

"We just gotta wait for the wife and kids to come down," Bob said, sitting down on one of the benches outside. He put ear buds in and pulled out his phone. I awkwardly stood next to him as he watched a basketball game on his phone, every now and then cheering for whoever was making the baskets. A few guests approached him and asked for an autograph. He obliged, almost unwillingly, and never bothered to take the ear buds out to actually talk to his fans.

The wife, Mrs. Bob, came down around 3:30 with two kids in tow. I stuck my hand out to introduce myself to Mrs. Bob, but she didn't have time for that. The kids shook my hand, though. They were cute. One boy and one girl.

"Where's your car?" Mom asked, handing me two backpacks to carry. I pointed towards my suburban on the far side of the lot. "Are you going to install the car seats or does someone from the hotel do that?"

I didn't have cars seats. I wasn't told to bring car seats. Judging by the age of the children, I also didn't need car seats for them, and Mom was mad that I hadn't thought to even bring them for her two children. Mom got one of the valet boys to get the car seats out of their own rental car, and handed them to me. It took me fifteen minutes to install both of them in the back row of the Suburban while Bob continued to watch basketball and occasionally sign an autograph.

The family had been to Disney World before but could not differentiate it from Universal Studios. Bob asked if he could ride The Hulk and I explained that was a different park. He looked confused for a second, and then went back to his basketball game not really caring either way. Mrs. Bob, however, had an itinerary planned out, and told me to drive to Animal Kingdom.

This was considered a PEP tour, because Bob was a highly recognizable person. I wouldn't necessarily recognize him, but anyone who follows sports most certainly would. With a PEP I had permission to park in otherwise off-limit locations, just to make it easier to maneuver in and out of crowds. I could have parked literally right in Africa to take this family to Safari, but I didn't today. I didn't really want to have to fight Safari trucks for parking spaces back there. I pulled in behind Rainforest Café and the family jumped out of the car.

"Do you have a stroller?" Mrs. Bob asked me.

"No, I didn't realize I needed one," I told her.

"We need a stroller. Also, don't you have those little soft toys for the kids?"

"Like… plush toys?"

"Yeah. Those. Like the Mickey and the Minnie ones?"

"No, I don't have any plush toys." Mrs. Bob gave me heavy shade. "Was I supposed to bring some?" I really didn't understand what Mom was getting at. Why was I supposed to bring gifts for the kids?

"The other tour guide always had toys for the kids." I knew that the family had a tour guide before me, and I guess that tour guide came with gifts of distinction for the kids. No one told me I had to hit a Target before the tour. I assumed the attractions in the park would take care of entertaining the kids. "Whatever. Where's the ride with all the animals?"

I hijacked a stroller hanging out backstage and had the kids sit in that. I decided I was going to push the stroller through the park, if only because that basically freed me from having to talk to Bob and Mrs. Bob. The only downside was that Bob stood about 6'6" so he was a walking beacon for attention. We barely moved fifteen feet into the park before someone spotted him and wanted a picture. He, still very much into his basketball game, paused for a second, mustered a smile, and we continued on.

As the tour guide, I was supposed to work as the bouncer for Bob. I was supposed to keep all other guests away from him so we could enjoy our stroll through Animal Kingdom. But while Bob stood 6'6", I stood 5'4", so there was no way I was going to fight anyone off who wanted to see him. Instead, Mrs. Bob had to do that. Mrs. Bob must have been used to doing that, because as soon as someone started approaching our group, she held up her hand and shooed them away. Mrs. Bob was fiercely intimidating. I wouldn't have wanted to mess with her either.

The most trouble we had walking came from the guests who would just yell at Bob, like "YO BOB, YOU SCORED THAT POINT!" or whatever sports fans yell at sports players. Bob honestly didn't hear most of these yells because there was still a basketball game to watch on his phone. Mrs. Bob led him through the park like a seeing-eye dog so he didn't trip over any strollers or benches while completely ignoring his surroundings.

There was no way I was about to put Bob into the standard queue line for Safari, or even the FastPass line. I didn't have to, anyway. I was allowed to head in the exit of this attraction because putting Bob in the close-quarters Safari queue was just a recipe for disaster; it was a disaster anytime someone recognizable went into that line. A disaster for anyone in any line, actually.

I pushed the stroller ahead up the hill and then down the hill and to the Safari unload area. One of the Cast Members there saw me coming. "Did you call ahead?" he asked.

"Was I supposed to call ahead?" I didn't really know. I wasn't doing PEP tours every week, so I was constantly forgetting how to do them. I was constantly telling other Cast Members it was my "first day" so I was going to need a little bit of help. In reality it was like my 547th day and I still didn't have the slightest idea how to enter into anything other than the actual queue line.

"Yeah, it's fine. I'll get you on the next truck." I parked the stroller and the kids jumped out and moved towards the exit area where they were supposed to load. The Safari truck pulled into the dock, and conveniently it happened to be a truck full of fans of Bob's sports team. Bob looked to Mrs. Bob. Mrs. Bob looked to me. Seriously, how was I supposed to know that the Safari truck was going to be full of college boys wearing Bob's team shirt?

I pulled the kids forward and brought them to the truck as Mrs. Bob fought her way through the crowd with Bob. He signed two autographs and took one picture, then he jumped into the truck and the Cast Member closed the gate on them.

"You're not riding?" Mrs. Bob asked me. I shook my head "no".

"I've got to make a phone call!" I lied. I didn't want to be stuck on Safari with them for twenty minutes. I really should have gone with them. It was probably a bad decision to put Bob on Safari without the proper supervision. I can only imagine what happened when they rolled into the loading dock and the entire queue saw him settled in the front seat. Now that's something I actually would have liked to witness.

Instead, I bought a banana, a diet Coke, a cream-cheese pretzel, and a cookie from the cart outside of the Safari, then I ducked behind a CAST MEMBERS ONLY fence, sat on the ground, and ate my makeshift lunch.

When they got off Safari I was told it was time to go to Hollywood Studios. Actually, Bob once again asked if he could ride The Hulk, and Mrs. Bob was like, yeah, that's the park we're going to next, and I was like, this is awkward guys, but that's not actually a place I can take you today. And Mrs. Bob was like, what do you mean we can't ride The Hulk? And I was like, well, technically Disney does own Marvel but... that's at Universal Studios and we're going to Hollywood Studios to ride Rock 'n' Roller Coaster and Bob looked completely uninterested in this and Mrs. Bob rolled her eyes and asked if the kids could ride it and I looked at the kids who were not 48" and I sighed. We trekked from Africa all the way back up to the front of the park, got in the car, and drove to Hollywood Studios.

I parked behind Tower of Terror like I always did and unloaded everyone from the car.

"Don't forget the autograph books!" Mrs. Bob yelled at Bob, who turned to look at me.

"Oh, are they in one of the backpacks?" I asked, reaching into the backseat of the car.

"Didn't you bring us autograph books?" Mrs. Bob asked.

"I didn't realize I needed to bring autograph books." Once again, I should have stopped at Target.

"How are the kids going to get autographs if they don't have autograph books?"

"We can go buy them in the park."

"So I have to pay for them?" Mrs. Bob was borderline disgusted with this notion. "Our other guide always brought the kids autograph books." I wanted to know who this other guide was, and why they were showering these kids with gifts when clearly Bob was making more money than I would make in my entire life. I asked the Office if they knew who Bob's prior guide had been; Mrs. Bob seemed to think the guide was named Doug. Their prior guide was actually a female named Susan so something had gotten lost in translation.

We entered into Studios right next to Rock 'n' Roller Coaster. The kids were way too short to ride, and I was not about to suggest a "rider switch" to Bob and Mrs. Bob. Besides, I could go up the exit, anyway.

"Could you tell unload that we're coming in? Just two riders," I whispered to the Cast Member standing at the queue entrance. He stared up at Bob; Bob stared down at his phone, still watching the basketball game, probably completely unaware that we had even entered into another park. The Cast Member nodded and we headed for the merchandise shop.

I led the family up the exit, through the shop, and towards the metal gates separating the unloading area of Coaster from the picture viewing area. One of the coordinators was already standing there waiting for me. "Just two?" he asked, staring at up Bob and Mrs. Bob who was busy looking at Aerosmith merchandise.

"Yeah. I've got these two," I said pointing down to the kids. "We're going to sit right here." The kids and I made ourselves comfy on the floor of the Coaster shop while Bob and Mrs. Bob rode twice.

"The Hulk was awesome!" Bob told me as he exited off.

Mrs. Bob informed me that it was time for dinner, and I was like, there are dinner reservations? She rolled her eyes and told me that dinner was at the buffet place with the characters, and I wanted to yell YOU COULD LITERALLY BE TALKING ABOUT FIFTEEN DIFFERENT PLACES. But she told me the place was in Studios, so that meant it was Hollywood and Vine. We headed over that way.

"Where can we get those books?" she asked as we walked.

"Autograph books?"

"Yeah, the books that you didn't have in the car." I pointed to a merchandise location and they went inside to go buy two autograph books and came out with two bags full of merchandise. Mrs. Bob put them in my arms. "Run these back to the car while we're eating."

I checked them into Hollywood and Vine. The seater looked at Bob, looming over all of us, and asked me if they should be seated off to the side of the restaurant. I wanted to tell the seater that they could sit in the middle of Echo Lake for all I cared. They were led inside and brought to a table in the far corner but directly in front of the windows. It wasn't even an issue, since Bob spent the entire meal staring down at his phone, so no one walking by outside knew it was him.

Meanwhile, I ran back to the car with the two giant bags of merchandise and put them in the back trunk. I stopped on my way back and got a burger, which I ate as I wandered backstage. I made it back to Hollywood and Vine in plenty of time, and they were still busy eating. So I went next door and got a peanut butter and jelly milkshake and chugged it while they finished dinner. They emerged about an hour and a half later.

"The kids didn't get to meet a lot of characters." Mrs. Bob said to me.

"We can go meet Lightning McQueen," I told her, because it was late in the day and by this point all other characters had already gone home for the evening.

"Who's that?" Mrs. Bob asked.

"He's a car."

"We can just go back to the hotel."

I loaded the family back into the car and drove them back to the hotel. I jumped out of the car, like I always did unloading guests, and ran around to let them out. The kids got out and waved goodbye to me, Mrs. Bob got out and thanked me for driving them, and Bob got out and looked up from his phone long enough to tell me that Michigan had won. Go team.

TWENTY-THREE

There was something magical about being paid to push a stroller around World Showcase on a warm spring day with a slight breeze. I was elated every time guests made the independent decision to stop and get something to eat from one of the little outdoor food carts, because that meant I had maybe four minutes to buy all the German pretzels I could manage and shove them into my little black tour bag for later. Sometimes there was a cheese booth set up. I was getting the cheese fondue platter in Germany for free and that was magical enough for me.

Often I'd find myself strolling, with a stroller, through World Showcase early in the afternoon, after just having finished up a lunch somewhere with my guests, and it was so peaceful and just *nice*. Mom and Dad would usually trail behind me, holding hands and talking to one of their children, while I entertained the one in the stroller, pointing out hidden Disney touches in the countries. I always find people describe EPCOT as the true park in the family of theme parks, because there's so much space to spread out and just sit and enjoy the weather and maybe some gelato.

But these nice moments never lasted long. By the time we made it to Japan, little Sally would be screaming like she was being skinned alive because she had been denied a patriotic themed Minnie plush, and the peaceful idea of sauntering around World Showcase was nothing more than a passing dream. I constantly had International Cast Members judging me because it was most definitely *my* fault that I brought a shrieking child into their pavilion.

Not all of my tours involved screaming children in faux countries. A majority of my tours were actually awesome tours, and I was always sad to leave a family at the end of the day. I found it hard to bond with families I was only with for six hours, because they were focused on getting in, riding all the rides, and getting out. There was no downtime for chitchat. However, with tours that would span all day, from breakfast to fireworks, or tours that went across multiple days, it was like I had been adopted into a surrogate family. Some families insisted I eat every meal with them, because I was part of *their* family now.

I did, though, have one family who told me I reminded them of their Aspen ski instructor, but the difference between the two of us lay with the fact that I ate lunch with them that afternoon. I guess the ski instructor never did.

It was always sad leaving a family that I really liked at the valet because I never knew if I was going to see them again. Sure, we had exchanged emails and the kids had found me on Facebook, but I wondered if they would take a trip down to hang out with me again. One dad told me they only took Disney vacations every four years, and asked what was the likelihood of me still being a guide four years in the future.

"I'll probably die here, wandering around the EPCOT parking lot, hopelessly looking for my car in the vast wasteland of pavement," I told him. And I only lost my car once in the EPCOT parking lot, but I never forgot the traumatizing experience of that summer day.

I never saw that family again. I hope they enjoy their next tour guide just as much.

I had a handful of repeat guests who I'd see maybe twice a year, if not more. One family visited so many times that I met all of their extended relatives including half brothers, half sisters, half aunts, uncles, and one brother from dad's third marriage who everyone treated like he was 100% blood related anyway. They were my favorite family. They were a family who insisted I eat with them for every meal, and always made sure I was riding rides with them because they hated the idea of me standing idly by waiting for them. I became friends with the teenagers, babysat the little ones while the parents went on thrill rides, and one of the pre-teens asked me how to become a tour guide because she wanted to be just like me when she grew up. She told me this as we were exiting Test Track and I know I welled up in the merchandise shop.

They were my absolute favorite family and they never handed me a wad of stickers. This was the family I loved so much I honestly didn't want them to thank me because I felt that would have been weird. I would have hung out with this family for free. They reminded me of my own family, and how our vacations functioned as dysfunctional as possible, and I loved them for that.

Once I didn't host them, and the mom sent me a text, asking why I wasn't around. I apologized to her again and again, but I had another commitment that I couldn't get out of. I assured her that another guide, just as good as I was, would step in and host them. I went so far as to ask the Office for a specific guide to host them, and the Office ignored my request and paired them with a big-mouthed, big-haired tour guide. At the conclusion of the tour the new guide complained to me that she hadn't gotten any stickers for the two days she spent with them.

Like any good fairytale, I guess being a tour guide was all about money.

TWENTY-FOUR

I never rode Tower of Terror. The word "terror" is right in the name; why would I subject myself to that? I don't like heights or drops, so I'd load my guests onto the attraction and sneak into the bypass elevator and make my way down to the unload area. I could sit down there.

The bypass elevator is literally just an elevator, and I used to hit the button to go down all by myself, and then one day a rude coordinator told me that I needed a Tower Cast Member to operate the elevator and that I couldn't wander around the building by myself. So now I waited for a Cast Member to show up to take me down to the ground floor to wait.

Off to the side I could see that there was a bellhop talking to some kids. I assumed he was trying to talk them into the ride and explain that it wasn't as scary as everyone made it out to be. But the kids did nothing but shake their head at the bellhop. I took a step closer to them, and realized that the kids didn't understand anything the bellhop was saying. The kids didn't speak English.

"What's happening?" I asked the bellhop, inserting myself into the situation.

"I think their dad is on the ride, but they can't wait for him here."

"What language do they speak?" The bellhop shrugged.

I looked at the little boys. One was clearly older than the other, and they held hands so they wouldn't get separated. The older boy told me something in hurried French. I recognized the word for "father".

"I speak a little French," I told the bellhop. I turned to the boys. "Je parle un peu le Français." I told them. They nodded. They had understood that.

The older boy said something hurried in French again. I didn't understand it. I only spoke a *little* French, and I could not differentiate one word from the other. The boy kept pointing at the elevator doors behind us, and I took that to mean that their father really was on the ride, and he had told them to wait here.

But how do I say, you can't wait here, your dad's exiting on the ground floor?

"Um. Ton père. Premier étage!" I have never been prouder of myself in my entire life than when I pulled the word "first floor" in French out of my brain. "Premier étage!"

The boys looked at one another. The bellhop looked at me. "What are you trying to say?"

"I'm trying to tell them that their father will be on the first floor. I know like six French words, okay? Give me a sec." I raced through my brain again. I held my hands out wide, gesturing to the themed basement area around us. "Deuxième étage. Ah! Avec moi, soirée, premier étage!"

"Nooooo." The boy said with his little French accent.

"Avec moi! Soirée! Premier étage! Soirée!"

"Nooooooo." The French boy said again.

"Seriously what are you telling them?" The bellhop asked.

"With me." I pointed to myself. I pointed down to the ground. "First floor. Exit. Ton père est soirée premier étage Avec moi soirée!"

The boys looked more and more confused with every French word I butchered. They said something in French. I understood none of it, like they understood my attempt at French. I tried Googling a longer sentence on my phone, but the reception in Tower of Terror is horrible. I couldn't get any bars. I went back to telling the boys that they could exit with me, first floor. I pointed to the elevator behind me. They shook their heads quickly.

"Oh, ça, uh…elevator. Elevator est…no…woosh!" I made dramatic hand gestures, conveying to the boys that the elevator behind us was not going to drop thirteen stories down to the ground. "Avec moi, no woosh! Avec moi, soirée, premier étage!"

Maybe the boys understood me; maybe they just wanted me to stop slaughtering their language. Either way they hesitantly took a few steps forward and peeked at the bypass elevator. The older one said something to the younger one, and then they said something to me, and we all got inside. "Bien!" I said to them once we were all inside. They nodded because they understood that word.

The elevator descended one whole flight down to the ground. We exited out the hallway and in-between the two elevator shafts. The boy's father was waiting around the corner for them.

"Sortie!" the boy yelled to me as soon as we got down to the exit. The father came over to me and shook my hand, said something to me in French just assuming I understood fluently, and the three of them went off. "Au revoir!" they yelled.

I managed to get a bar of reception in the basement of Tower, and googled the French words I had been saying to the boys. I kept on telling them *soirée*, but soirée is not the word for exit. Sortie is. I wasn't telling the boys to exit with me on the first floor. I was telling them to come party with me on the first floor. Soiree. A party.

Avec moi. Soirée! Premier étage. I probably scarred those poor French boys for life.

TWENTY-FIVE

Sometimes I accidentally signed up to work overtime. It was one of those instances when the Office had sent out an email saying that they had tours to fill, and if we weren't already scheduled to work we should pick one up for easy overtime. Okay, easy overtime. That's something I can get on board with. I emailed the Office, and I was immediately put on a tour for the following week. Two days before the tour I was sent an email regarding the tour from one of the coordinators at the Office. The tour seemed easy enough. Nine guests, six hours in Magic Kingdom.

The day before the tour I was at the gym when I got an email. I read it quickly on a treadmill, skimming the words for tour details. One detail stuck out. "Wheelchair." The dad was in a wheelchair. Honestly, the information didn't faze me. I had done plenty of tours before where one of the guests had been in either a wheelchair or an ECV due to mobility issues. It wouldn't be the first time I had handled it, and it wouldn't be the last.

I showed up at the Office the morning of the tour right around 8am, with my iced coffee in hand and my sunglasses on my head. I breezed in and began my morning pre-tour rituals of getting my car, getting my keys, getting more coffee, when from somewhere in a cubicle I heard someone call, "IS THAT ANNIE?"

I moved towards the sound of the voice. It was the coordinator who had assigned me the tour. She pulled me into her cubicle space.

"So your tour today," she starts. "It might be challenging."

"You emailed me yesterday about the wheelchair, it's perfectly fine. I've had plenty of guests in wheelchairs before."

"Dad is a non-transferable."

"What?" The word was one I recognized, but her phrasing didn't make sense.

"Dad. Non-transferable."

"He's in a wheelchair."

"Yeah, and he can't transfer out of it."

I started at this coordinator. Slowly I was putting the pieces together, but this coordinator took me for stupid and explained it to me anyway. "He can't get out of his wheelchair, Annie. You're going to have to figure out how to deal with that."

"You couldn't have told me this yesterday? Or two days ago?"

"I thought you would have called in."

"I wouldn't have called in. I'm not a guide like *that*." Sometimes if guides heard that their tour was going to be difficult, or wouldn't tip, they'd call in. It was kind of a low blow.

The coordinator didn't seem to hear anything I was saying. She went about deleting emails from her inbox. "I think he was active military or something? I only talked to the mom and she didn't say. He doesn't have any legs."

This wasn't a big issue, honestly. It was just a super rude move on the coordinator's part to drop it on me at 8:17am when I have to meet the guests at 9am. I would have liked to actually prepare for a tour like this. Yes, I know the attractions at Magic Kingdom are wheelchair accessible, but it would have been nice to refresh my memory so I knew quickly off the top of my head which ones we could or couldn't do today. But something like that would have been too much trouble for that coordinator.

I drove to Magic Kingdom and chugged a diet coke as I went.

The family was supposed to meet me at 9am on the steps of City Hall and I saw them coming from a mile away. They were dressed in bright blue t-shirts and I asked why they hadn't brought me one.

"We've got some back at the room!" Mom excitedly told me as she introduced the family. She had me meet her two children (who told me they designed the t-shirts themselves), then her parents, then her husband's parents, and then her husband's brother. Lastly, I met her husband, Dad, who was confined to a wheelchair. He didn't have legs, and he also didn't have a right arm. Instead, he had a prosthetic hand that he used to maneuver his motorized wheelchair around. He wore a backwards baseball hat and shook my hand with his able hand.

"Today's going to be a great day!" He smiled.

I realized it was at this point I had one of two options to carry out the tour. I could either drastically tiptoe around the fact that Dad was in a wheelchair and needed to be assisted onto every ride (and then assisted off, of course), or I could ask him, straight up, what he could and couldn't do so we could work together to make it the best day ever. I went with the second option.

"What do you and do you not feel comfortable riding?" I asked him as we made our way down Main Street. It really wasn't my decision what he could and couldn't ride; it was completely up to him. No, I couldn't physically assist him in or out of any ride vehicles, but I could help him with every other aspect of the day.

"Nothing that goes upside down," Dad laughed. "I want to ride everything else."

Challenge: accepted.

We went to Fantasyland first; the boys were young and I knew the quicker we could get in and out of that land the better. The wheelchair was bulky, and as the day grew more and more crowded I knew it might pose a problem navigating through crowds with such a large group. We headed for "small world" first. As we turned the corner down the wheelchair entrance, I could see the wheelchair boat three away from the dock. It was like a sign from the heavens.

I loaded the family onto "small world", and the boys thought it was awesome that there was a boat to accommodate their dad. They sat in the front seats, and Dad sat directly behind them, and I watched them sail away on the happiest cruise that ever sailed.

I then ran as fast as I could out of "small world" and towards the Fantasyland managers Offices, where I knew my friend Tony was currently working. I didn't even make it to the manager's Offices; Tony was strolling around the Carrousel courtyard with his pickers in hand. He saw me run at him, like a bat out of hell, or a tour guide out of "small world".

"What's up, kid?" he asked, as I panted, breathless, in front of him.

"Do you know the wheelchair accessible rides in Magic Kingdom?"

Tony cocked an eyebrow at me. "Shouldn't you know that?"

"No, like the ones where they HAVE to transfer," I said, collecting myself. I had braided my hair into French braids that morning, and I could already feel they were falling out of place. "My dad's in a wheelchair. He can't transfer out. So, like, Space Mountain is a no-go, right?"

Tony led me to the tiny Peter Pan break room. There really is a tiny Peter Pan break room, which is just like a tiny hallway next to the exit of the ride where there are four chairs and a refrigerator, and that's where Peter Pan Cast Members have to take their break while they listen to Peter defeat Hook over and over again on loop. Tony disappeared behind a door and emerged a moment later with a Magic Kingdom Disability Map.

"I've got one of those," I said, pulling my map out of my bag. I had taken one from the Office. "But can he ride Speedway? Can he ride Dumbo?"

"He can't ride Pan," Tony gestured to the ride behind him. "Well, he can. But we can't stop the belt."

"Why?"

"They'll have to pick him up and carry him to a ship. If we stop the belt there's a chance it won't restart and then it'll go 101." Peter Pan is one of the original Magic Kingdom attractions. I swear it hasn't seen a proper refurbishment since 1971.

I lay my head against the wall and looked at my watch. I still had about four minuets until they'd unload from "small world".

Tony pulled out his radio and started calling all the other managers of all the other lands in Magic Kingdom. He confirmed that my guest could ride Speedway, and Space if he really wanted. With Space he had to fit underneath the restraint safely, with about 4' of some appendage underneath. It seemed difficult, but I bet Dad was going to want to try it anyway.

I went back to meet my guests at "small world", and before they exited Tony had heard from all of the other managers, too. I assumed there was a wheelchair boat at Pirates that Dad could wheel right onto, and Tony was quick to remind me, "There's a drop there, Annie. How much fun would it be to then fish guests out of the water?"

Not fun at all, Tony.

My guests exited up the ramp at "small world", excited for what was next. I suggested Winnie the Pooh, but the kids had already seen Peter Pan nestled directly across the way from us. There was no gain in avoiding the subject. I turned to the parents. "We can totally go ride Peter Pan, but unfortunately they can't stop the moving walkway for us. So you'll have to be lifted out and placed onto one of the ships."

Dad seemed completely cool with this, and Grandpa and Uncle were more than willing to life him out of the chair. So over to Peter Pan we went, snaking through the tiny queue line until we came to a stop just at the beginning of the moving walkway. I unhooked the chains, while Grandpa and Uncle lifted Dad up out of his chair and quickly and safely carried him to his awaiting pirate ship. One of the kids climbed in with him.

As they sailed away to Neverland, I took a thirty-second breather. "Where to?" Dad asked as soon as everyone was out.

The best part about some of the newer attractions at Magic Kingdom is that a lot of them have wheelchair accessible vehicles. So guess who has to transfer? No one. No one has to transfer for rides like Winnie the Pooh or Ariel or Buzz Lightyear or even Jungle Cruise. They all have a wheelchair accessible vehicle and it's fascinating seeing them work. Dad just rolled right onto both Pooh and Ariel, and the Cast Members there were completely accommodating and helpful about making sure that everyone was safely inside the vehicles. They saw wheelchair guests way more often than I did. I know Mom loved every second of it because I could tell she had been a little worried about making this trip. Dad and the kids were riding Teacups (no, there was no wheelchair teacup, but there was a teacup with an extra wide door that swiveled out so Dad could seamlessly move from his wheelchair into the teacup) and Mom and I were standing over at the attraction's exit gate. I had pointed the grandparents in the direction of the bathroom and they had gone off in search of that.

"The community raised money for us to come down here, it's really a marvelous thing," she said, pointing to her shirts. "The boys designed these, and we sold them as fundraisers, too."

"It's so awesome seeing them all together. I'm so proud of Disney World for being completely accommodating," I said, pointing to the family spinning round and round on a teacup.

"After his accident I never would have dreamed of taking a vacation like this. But here we are!" Mom beamed. The ride slowly came to a stop, and one of the Cast Members went rushing over with Dad's wheelchair for him to climb back into. "If I could just ask one favor?"

"Sure, what?" I expected Mom to ask whether we could we meet Mickey or ride down Main Street in a parade float or parasail over the Seven Sea's Lagoon.

"Could we avoid trains today?" she said simply.

"Uh, sure." I replied, not understanding what trains had to do with anything.

"It's just..." Mom trailed off, trying to find words. "His accident. He was a train engineer. That's how his accident happened. A train hit him. I know he's okay with trains now, but I get nervous that the boys aren't. I'm not okay with trains."

Want to know who loved trains? Walt Disney.

Want to know what place is full of trains? Magic Kingdom.

Walt loved trains from a very early age. It was a childhood hobby of his. But as he grew older, he grew out of trains and completely forgot about them for a while. Then Walt started working with a man named Ward Kimball. Ward loved trains more than Walt ever had. Ward loved trains so much that he had a life-size replica of a steam train in his backyard. Don't worry, Ward's wife loved trains, too. And the two of them would go and ride around their life-size replica train in their backyard, and they could go forwards in the train, and they could go backwards in the train, and that was it.

Walt was really jealous of Ward's train. Walt wanted a train of his own. Know who didn't like trains? Walt's wife, Lillian. Lillian wanted nothing to do with trains. Lillian had this beautiful picturesque window overlooking her backyard, and she didn't want to have to sit by the window playing cards with her friends and watch Walt ride by on his silly train. Walt agreed to compromise on his train, though. He built a tunnel for the train to travel through and that's what Lillian's window overlooked. She could stare at her beautiful gardens, and know that somewhere in the mound of dirt Walt's train was riding around and around. The train was called the Carolwood Pacific because their house was on Carolwood Drive. You'll see a lot of things called "Carolwood" scattered around Disney World. The train station in Fantasyland behind Barnstormer is the Carolwood Station.

Walt's love of trains spread through Disneyland Railroad, and traveled down to Florida, too, with the Walt Disney World Railroad. Purchasing the trains was one of the last things Walt did before he passed away. Trains are always going to be a part of Disney history and now that was the only thing I needed to avoid today.

There was no way I could take this family anywhere near Frontierland.

I led the family from the Teacups to the Speedway and I got them all cars (five cars in total), and while they rode around the track, I chugged a mocha smoothie from Auntie Gravity's and ate a banana as quickly as I could. I led the family to Space Mountain and I held my breath for 2:41 seconds while Dad rode Space with the oldest boy. Dad loved Space, the boy did not. Buzz was simple because Dad could load on and off the wheelchair vehicle with ease. We made our way down Main Street, went to go see Mickey (and the princesses for Mom and the grandmas), and we came back up Main Street and headed into Adventureland. The tour was only supposed to last six hours, and that was my max time for them. I had to leave them at six hours, which meant I had to stall so we never made it to Frontierland.

Aladdin's Magic Carpets, Jungle Cruise, Pirates, and then I backtracked a little and took the family towards Haunted Mansion. As we walked, I could tell that the boys were looking off in the Wild West direction.

"Isn't there a log flume here?" Uncle asked me as we gathered around Haunted Mansion.

"Um, yeah. But isn't it a little cold to ride that today? And you guys will get completely soaked," I said, ushering everyone into the queue.

"I want to get soaked!"

"Me too!" the boys cried excitedly. I looked over at Splash Mountain in Frontierland. I could easily take them there and let them ride that. But per Mom's request, I couldn't take them anywhere near the wildest ride in the wilderness. I told Mom this. I told Mom that there was in fact a log flume attraction, but it was next to the runaway train rollercoaster. She didn't look too pleased hearing that the attraction was referred to as a "runaway train".

The boys stayed adamant about riding Splash Mountain. As soon as kids got an idea of an attraction in their head it was little to no use trying to talk them out of it. We hiked to Splash after Haunted Mansion. Dad looked over at Thunder Mountain. "What's that?" he asked.

"It's a really scary rollercoaster. Two loops." Dad gave me a look that told me I could drop the act. "It's a train rollercoaster."

"Cool! I want to try that!" he said, and there was no use trying to talk him out of that, either.

Everyone got off Splash soaked, as I had predicted, and we fought through the massive crowd in Frontierland towards the front of Thunder. The Thunder queue, though it just went through a refurbishment, is still not designed to accommodate wheelchairs. So wheelchair parties have to enter through the exit. The Cast Member stationed there saw us coming and quickly asked me how many were riding. I was prepared to wait ten minutes or so for us to be loaded on, but the Cast Member took the family right away.

Now, if you're familiar with Thunder Mountain, you'll know there are two loading docks. A right side and a left side. If you're in the queue, the right side is where the wheelchairs load. It's got a little holding pen where wheelchairs can be stored, and the last car of all trains is designed to accommodate guests transferring out of the wheelchair and into the train. The last row has a little swivel door, like at Dumbo and Teacups, where it opens, and then Dad could just scoot from one into the other. The Cast Member in the tower then has to know that there's a wheelchair party riding, and direct the train back to the correct dock so Dad could then unload from the runaway train and back into his wheelchair. The other side of the dock wasn't large enough to accommodate the space of a wheelchair.

By this time in the day it was hot, I was tired, and I knew I was getting completely dehydrated. The only things I had eaten were the banana and the mocha smoothie. Thunder Mountain is only about a three-minute ride from start to finish, but I knew I was on the verge of passing out. I had been so focused on the family, and making sure that everything was running smoothly, that I had completely forgotten to drink enough water. I watched the family load onto Thunder, the train dispatched, and I ran out the exit and towards the popcorn cart outside. They had Gatorade.

There was a line there; because of course there was a line the one time I needed to get Gatorade quickly. I stationed myself at the end of the popcorn line, and waited, and waited, and after what felt like forever I bought my Gatorade and chugged it as quickly as possible. It was a blue Gatorade, and halfway through chugging it the thought crossed my mind that I was drinking it took quickly and that if I spilled any on myself it was going to stain my white shirt blue. I took a breather from chugging and looked up to see that one of the grandmas was standing right in front of me.

"Oh, gosh, are you guys off already?" I asked her, as we walked back towards the exit.

"Everyone else is riding again. Once was enough for me!" Grandma laughed.

The family exited a few minutes later. The boys came rushing up to me, excited. "That was awesome! We rode it three times!"

"Three times?" I questioned. I looked to one of the parents for confirmation, and Uncle nodded.

"They let us two more times!" he said, also excited.

I looked to the Cast Member standing at the exit and he meekly shrugged his shoulders. The family moved down the exit ramp as the Cast Member leaned in to me, "We sent them to the wrong dock. Twice. Couldn't let them unload since the wheelchair was on the other side."

So, the one attraction I was supposed to avoid they ended up riding three times in a row because the tower Cast Member failed to see that they went to the left side dock twice, when they needed to end up on the right.

Shortly after that we hit the six-hour mark and I had to leave the family for the day. I brought them over to a late lunch at Liberty Tree Tavern and told them their lunchtime would line up perfectly with the parade if they wanted to see that. The family was incredibly appreciative of everything I had done for them during the day, but honestly I hadn't done much of anything. All I did was double check with each Cast Member at each attraction to make sure that their procedures allowed for Dad to ride. The family really did the rest.

Working in Magic Kingdom I found myself constantly getting grief from other guests about the fact that the park was unaccommodating for guests traveling in wheelchairs. And I always used to say, "Listen. This one time I had a tour where the dad had no legs and no arm and he rode *every single ride* in the park, including the one Mom told me that he wasn't allowed to ride."

I think this was a case of the triumph of the human spirit.

TWENTY-SIX

It started out like any normal tour. 9am pick up at the Animal Kingdom Lodge. I just wish that guests would have told me at hour one that they were going to yell at me at hour eleven in Magic Kingdom.

I was running late, as usual, but I also anticipated my guests to run late, as usual, too. I pulled up to the valet at 8:25am. They were nowhere in sight.

One of the valet boys pointed for me to park my van on the far side of the valet, and I ignored his wishes and stopped right in the center of it. "How about I just give you the keys and you do whatever you want with this van?" I asked, and he laughed as he jumped behind the wheel to move my giant mini-bus.

I always found the DAKL valet area to be tiny and cramped. I always felt that for the size of the resort, and the amount of people constantly coming and going, their main entrance into the hotel could have been bigger. This always made it seem like there were a lot more people hanging around then there really were.

From across the valet I saw a tall lanky boy dart between cars and began signaling for them to move forward. I squinted my eyes in the Florida sun and saw a mop of brown hair and thin wire frame glasses.

I hadn't seen him for at least nine months. I honestly just assumed he had left the company and had gone on to do something else with his life. But here he was, standing before me, parking cars at the DAKL. I didn't know what to do. Should I wave to him? Should I go over and say hi? Do I just stand here and pretend to be talking to a guest?

I looked back in Trevor's direction, but he had already disappeared behind a car again. I had lost the moment.

Then, like magic, the cars parted, the Voices of Liberty sang, ticker tape fell from the valet ceiling, and Trevor made his way over to where I was standing. He didn't come all the way to me, because he was in the process of trying to move another car, but he came forward so much that we made eye contact for a split second. He waved. He remembered me!

It took another three or four cars before Trevor had a moment to come over and actually say hi. He sauntered over, his black tie waving in the wind against his purple shirt. "Hey, how are you?" he asked, taking a spot next to me.

"I'm good, how are you? I didn't realize you were over here now."

"I was transferred," he said, running a hand through his slicked back brown hair. "This place isn't as crazy as the Grand Flo." He laughed, and I laughed too because we were both thinking back to all those times we were stuck at the Grand Floridian.

This was Trevor's and my big moment to be reunited, like Nemo and Marlin, and my guests promptly interrupted it.

The mom came over to me and stuck my hand out. I shook it.

"Oh, I'll go grab your car," Trevor told me, as he rushed away through the valet to grab my van.

The mom introduced me to her family. It was her and her two adult sisters, one maybe in her mid-30s, and the other who was surprisingly my age. Then it was Mom's three kids, ranging in ages from 8 to 13.

"We've been looking forward to this all week!" she said to me as Trevor pulled up in my big white van and parked it. He jumped out of the front seat and ran around to the side to open the giant double doors to let everyone in. He followed me around to the driver's side.

"Do you know when you'll be done?" he asked, opening my door and sticking his hand out. I grabbed it as he gently assisted me into the driver's seat.

"With my luck, probably never." I whispered back. He shut my door and waved goodbye. I did the same.

"Is that your boyfriend?" Mom asked from the back seat.

"No, he's just a friend." I told her.

"He's cute. I like that nerdy look," she said to her sisters, who both nodded in agreement.

For some reason, this family gave off a warm and friendly vibe. The mom seemed pretty cool, her adult sisters seemed cool, and the kids didn't strike me as being a handful. My tour guide sense tingled, and I felt like, yeah, this should be a pretty good day! Lets make friends with this new family.

"I've known him for a while," I sighed, turning on my signal to pull out of the DAKL parking lot. "I haven't seen him in months, though. I feel like I'm blushing. Am I blushing?"

"No, but now you're flustered!" one of the sisters laughed, and everyone laughed, and I laughed, and I thought, what could possibly go wrong in about eleven hours?

We went to Animal Kingdom first.

"We didn't park here last time," Mom informed me as I pulled in behind Rainforest Café.

"Oh, you've had a tour before?" I said, surprised. No one had told me that this was a return tour for another guide.

"The last guide drove us right to Safari."

Again. *Our last guide...* "Our procedures have changed. We can no longer drive back behind Safari since it's such a congested area, with all the parade floats and the Safari vehicles."

Mom nodded like she understood. The family and I trekked through the park and back to the Safari, and then we went to Everest, and then Mom asked me if I could drive Older Aunt back to the hotel because she wasn't feeling good. She had been dehydrated earlier in the week, and Mom didn't want that to happen again.

Of course we could take her back to the hotel. Know who would still be at the hotel? Trevor.

I pulled up, and Trevor was waiting outside as if he knew I was coming back for him. He rushed at my van and grabbed my driver's side door. "I knew you'd come back to me." He said, smiling wide.

"I'm just dropping off!" I yelled at him, signaling for him to grab the passenger door instead. He realized I didn't have time to flirt right now, and hurried to the passenger side to grab the door.

"Everything alright?" he asked.

"I'm just coming back to rest for a bit," Aunt told him, as he held out his hand to help her out of the giant van. "Annie will pick me back up later!"

"I'll be waiting." Trevor waved goodbye to me, and I waved back, and my van full of guests gave a collective "awwwwww" as I pulled away from him. Trevor kind of looked like Milo from *Atlantis: The Lost Empire*.

"You should ask him out!" Mom told me.

"Oh no, I couldn't do that. I'm not that bold." I mumbled, as I once again drove away from the hotel.

"He's totally into you!" Middle Aunt gushed. If the guests could see it, there must be something there that wasn't there before.

I drove the family to EPCOT and we unloaded behind Soarin'. "Where are we having dinner?" Mom asked as we made our way into the building.

"I was told dinner would be at Prime Time."

Mom seemed to agree with this statement. "What time?"

"5pm."

"That'll work," she said, and we got into the queue.

When we were waiting in line for Test Track, Mom turned to me and asked, "Where are we watching the parade?"

"What parade?"

"The 3 o'clock parade."

This was one of those instances where a guest said something to me, and I was like, seriously, what are you talking about. We are standing in EPCOT and we've just discussed how we were going to Studios for dinner. How do you think we're going to fit the 3 o'clock parade in there, too? I looked down at my watch. It was just about 12:30pm. I hadn't asked for parade viewing from the Office, because I didn't think we needed parade viewing from the Office. That was one of my biggest tour pet peeves. Guests would just say things to me as if I had already anticipated their every need. No, I had no idea you wanted parade viewing, so I didn't book it.

"I didn't know you guys wanted to see the parade!" I laughed, because it was better than crying in the Test Track queue.

"Of course we want to see the parade!" Mom exclaimed, and the kids joined in cheering, too. I ushered the guests on Test Track and I hurried out the exit to send an e-mail to the Office.

The Office responded quickly with a YES. Phew. So that was at least dealt with in a timely manner.

The guests exited off Test Track and I told them the good news, that I had secured parade viewing for them! Yay! Everyone cheered as we headed out of the building. Mom wanted to stop somewhere for lunch, quickly, and I managed to talk her into heading to the Electric Umbrella, since it was the closest, and only, quick service around. I was not about to trudge into World Showcase knowing that I needed to make a parade at 3pm.

We finished lunch at Electric Umbrella and I hurried everyone back towards the van. We loaded in, and I started driving on my course to Magic Kingdom when...

"Can we swing by Animal Kingdom Lodge?"

I looked in the rear view mirror at Mom. She had her phone out and was clearly texting the sister back at the hotel. I looked at my clock. It was just after 2pm. I needed to be at Magic Kingdom by 2:30 at the latest or I'd lose my parade spot.

"Okay." I said, because I wasn't about to tell Mom that we were under a time crunch.

So back to DAKL I drove, and I pulled up to the valet and Trevor was standing there, waving me forward to park. "I didn't realize you missed me that much," he smirked, as he grabbed my driver's door.

"Someone in this van loves you!" Little Billy yelled from the back seat and Trevor cocked an eyebrow at me as the family jumped out of the car without any assist from either of us.

"We're just picking someone up," I said, wondering if my cheeks were rosy red.

The family hurried out of the car and into the hotel as I weakly yelled after them, "But we have a parade!" None of them heard me. They disappeared inside. I looked at my watch. 2:15pm.

"Rough day?" Trevor asked, leaning against the side of my van. He looked at his watch. "It's been about five hours."

"I hope there's only an hour left. Parade and *done*," I told him. I could potentially just leave them at the six-hour mark. I could tell them that they had only booked a tour for six hours, and my time was done so have fun without me for the rest of the day!

I sat in my car and nervously watched time tick away. The family had requested parade, I had booked the parade, and now we were dangerously close to missing the parade. Trevor went back to park cars and I prayed the family would come down any second. I thought about giving Trevor my number, but I didn't know if I could do that without drawing attention from every single other Cast Member standing at the DAKL valet. It was too risky. Maybe I could just get Little Billy to awkwardly slip it to him like a school Valentine.

But this couldn't be on the forefront of my mind. I needed to get these guests out of the hotel and to Magic Kingdom as quickly as possible. If everything went according to my plan, we'd be there for 2:45, barely. From there we would need to run from the Plaza gate all the way over to the Liberty Square bridge, or we'd be cut off and stuck watching the parade like all the other guests.

The family came downstairs at 2:30.

I yelled for them to get into my van, and they slowly climbed in, now wearing new outfits and carrying new bags with Middle Aunt in tow, telling me she was feeling much better.

"See you in a bit?" Trevor called to me, as I shut the doors behind the family.

"Hope so!" I ran around to my driver's side door, but he beat me to it.

"I'll be waiting," He held out a hand to help me in, and I grabbed it. It was quite the gentleman move. The family saw.

"Annie, you have to give him your number," the family scolded me as I drove as quickly as possible to Magic Kingdom. "You guys would be so cute together!"

"Lets get to parade first, and then we can talk about Trevor!" I laughed through gritted teeth as I barreled down World Drive in a small, tank-like 15 passenger van. We made it into Magic Kingdom at 2:50pm and I made them run from the Plaza Gate to the Liberty Square bridge. Surprisingly, there were still spots on the benches for them.

I leaned against the rail behind them, exhausted and stressed. This was not my idea of a fun organized tour. The parade passed us with all its magical whimsy, and the kids waved to characters, and Mom took pictures, and everyone had a nice time. I thought about the closest location to get a diet Coke.

I moved back to the family and stood behind the bench they were sitting on. "Did everyone like that?" I asked the kids, who smiled and giggled because who doesn't love a parade?

"Are we watching the parade from here tonight?" Mom asked.

I stared at her. What parade tonight? I decided to play dumb. "I didn't know we were watching the parade tonight!"

"That's why we hired you," Mom replied, coolly. "We want to watch the parade from the best seats."

Everyone else on the bridge begins to clear out and after a few minutes it's just me and my guests still lingering around. Mom discusses plans for the rest of the day, which don't include ending after six hours. She's still intent on having dinner over at Studios, so we can go and do all the rides there, and then coming back to Magic Kingdom in the evening to see the parade.

We begin to make our way through the throngs of guests trying to move post-parade. Mom's now in the lead, taking us behind the Castle and into Fantasyland. I've got my Blackberry out, furiously typing an email to the Office.

> Hey. It's Annie. Guess the Red family wants to see parade tonight, already assumes I've got seating. Please tell me there's still space in the first parade.

The Office responded:

Do your guests have tickets for tonight?

Of course my guests have tickets for tonight. We're standing in the park right now. I swiped their tickets into Animal Kingdom already. They have valid admission.

It takes me the walk from the Castle to Dumbo to register why the guests might need separate admission for tonight. It's a Tuesday. In December. That means that tonight there's a Christmas party, so the park closes at 7pm, and there'll be a Christmas parade at 8:15 and 10:30.

The kids ride Dumbo and I stand next to Mom, trying to figure out how to ask her about tonight. She clearly doesn't have tickets. I bet she doesn't even realize she needs separate admission tickets for tonight. I can't reserve parade viewing for them until I know if they have tickets. The Office won't let me hold spots for guests if there's a chance they might not go. After much thought, I take a deep breath. "Do you know if your tickets include admission for the Christmas party tonight?"

"You can just charge them to the room," Mom says, waving to a kid high above us in the air. I know for a fact that no general admission ticket to Disney World includes admission into any special parties, but it's the easiest way to broach the subject. Mom hands me her Key to the World Card, like I can do the transaction standing at Dumbo.

I email the Office back, telling them to buy tickets for the guests for the evening, and then beg for parade viewing.

> You got lucky, party's not sold out! Bridge is full, you guys are at firehouse.

I don't mind watching parades at the firehouse. I know most guests dislike it because there isn't any place to sit, but it's 90% of the time completely in the shade, and with the way the parade turns it's a wonderful view of every single float. It's a large space so the characters can come right up to the rope to shake hands and give hugs. Also, the Firehouse is directly next to City Hall, which means I can go inside and lie down on the VIP couch for fifteen minutes.

I tell Mom that I've secured party tickets for the family and that we've got parade viewing as well. She's pleased with the news, and we continue on our day. We finish up in Magic Kingdom, and then head over to Studios for dinner. I opt out of eating at Prime Time with them, and instead sit behind Star Tours eating a cheeseburger and fries.

After dinner I piled the family back into my 15-passenger van and we drive back to Magic Kingdom for the second time that day. By the time we arrived it was already dark, and the kids requested to ride Splash and Thunder before the parade. We stopped by City Hall, I printed out their Christmas party tickets, and then activated the tickets and got them Christmas party wristbands. We headed down Main Street and turned into Adventureland, heading towards Frontierland.

We rode Splash and Thunder.

By the time we were off those attractions it was almost time for the parade. I wanted to make sure my guests got a good spot, so we crossed through Fronterieland and into Liberty Square. With everything that had happened that day, I completely forgot that our parade viewing was at the Firehouse, not on the bridge. I approached the bridge anyway.

There was a little bit of chaos happening on the bridge. A coordinator I recognized by the name of Tom stood by the rope, talking to four other parade Cast Members. They were having a heated discussion, and I waited a second to interrupt and ask who was in charge of VIP viewing.

There was a lull in their conversation. I took it as an opportunity. "Excuse me, I'm checking the Red family in?" I asked the group of them.

Tom rolled his eyes and pulled a piece of paper out of his chest pocket. "Are you sure you guys have viewing?" he asked, looking over his sheet.

"Yeah, I reserved it earlier in the day."

"You guys aren't here on the bridge. You're at Firehouse," he scolded me, assuming I was one of the many other tour guides (and guests) who had already tried to weasel their way into parade viewing on the bridge.

I didn't realize that Mom was standing right behind me. "*What?*"

Tom looked at Mom. "Your viewing is down at the firehouse," he said to her. Then he turned to me. "And we've taken so many callouts today I know no one's taped it off yet."

"*What?*" Mom asked again, only halfway understanding our conversation.

"What do you mean no one's taped it off yet?" I asked Tom, getting closer to him so Mom couldn't hear us. But Tom decided to be less than a star Cast Member at that point in time.

"You're going to have to get tape from someone and block off space yourself."

"No one is down there in charge of viewing?"

"That's what I just said. Go make space for yourself down there."

I stared at Tom. I had encountered rude Cast Members before, but none of them had ever told me, in front of my guests, that I was going to need to tape off my own viewing area. He turned his back to me and restarted the conversation with his Cast Members that I had interrupted.

Mom stood dangerously close to me. I knew she had heard everything said between Tom and me. "What was he talking about?"

I turned to face her. I found this mom to be a much taller woman that I was used to, with short choppy dirty blonde hair and from everything that had already happened today I found her to be a little bit mean. The last thing I wanted to do was make her mad, but we were well beyond that point now.

"Our viewing area is down at the Firehouse..." I began, but she cut me off.

"There are plenty of seats here!" she yelled, gesturing to the bridge. It had about ten people on it so far. The Office only liked to put about twenty guests on it, so the area didn't feel cramped. I was once on the bridge for 43 guests and I assumed it was going to collapse and we were all going to fall into the lagoon around the Castle.

There were in fact a lot of empty benches on the bridge right now. Only ¾ of the front row had been taken up. Two more rows sat behind that.

"This area is reserved," Tom turned around to yell at Mom and me. There was no way I was getting on the bridge with him standing right in front of us.

I had no choice but to lead the family away from the bridge and down Main Street towards the Firehouse. Mom yelled the entire time about how unorganized the tour had been, how I was an unorganized tour guide, and how her last tour guide had everything planned out ahead of time so they didn't run into any bumps like this. I stopped listening to her by the time we reached Center Street. I turned to the to adult sisters and told them to stay back with the family while I ran ahead to the Firehouse to see what was happening there.

Chaos, is what was happening.

It was close to 8pm, which meant that the parade would be starting soon from Frontierland. It would take about 45 minutes for it to reach Main Street, but by that time every single spot along the parade route would be gone. All the spots along the parade route were already gone. Guests and their kids and their kid's strollers lined all up and down the pavement, and the area usually reserved for VIP viewing was packed with weary guests.

Mom knew what was happening. She knew that there wasn't any reserved space, and she knew that there was no way I was about to make guests move to make way for us, and she knew that I was quickly losing control of the situation. "This is ridiculous, take us back to the hotel," she demanded, standing on the Emporium corner.

"No, I can go and get us an area…"

"Annie, don't bullshit me. There's no space here. Get one of your managers on the phone."

"There's unfortunately no one in the Office at this hour." Yes, but there was still the tour coordinator on duty. However, I was not about to call him and explain that I was standing in Magic Kingdom with an irate guest upset over her parade viewing. "What can I do to fix this right now?"

"I don't even want to see the parade anymore. Take us back to the hotel. I'll be demanding a full refund for the tour." If there's one thing that never happened, it was this. Guests were never refunded for the tour. I picked the guests up at 9am, and it was just past 8pm. We had been out for eleven hours. There's no way the Office was going to give them today for free. I'd still get paid, sure, but the Office would be furious.

"I don't…" I started, but Mom knew I had nothing else to say. There was no space for us to watch the parade at Firehouse.

"Just take us back, Annie. I'll deal with your managers tomorrow."

I hung my head as I led them from the Emporium corner to the Tony's gate and we disappeared backstage. I looked at my watch. It was 8:20. The parade had started in Frontierland. I had one last option.

"Wait here. Wait right here. Don't go anywhere," I told the family. I made the ridiculously bold decision to leave my family backstage. No, I was too timid to slip Trevor my phone number on a DSA business card, but I was about to leave guests completely unattended in a backstage area because they were threatening to demand a full refund for my tour service.

I ran from the Plaza Gate out into Main Street. I ran down Main Street, following the parade route, in front of the Castle and to the bridge. As I ran I wondered what guests waiting for the parade thought of me. This tiny little tour guide, completely frazzled and out of sorts running as fast as her flat feet would take her trying to save a tour in the eleventh hour, literally. I made it to the bridge, completely out of breath. I hunched over and leaned against the rail. There was a tour guide standing on the other side of the rope who immediately jumped up like he knew something was horribly wrong.

"I need…who's in charge?" I panted.

"I don't know." The tour guide's name was Adam. "Are you okay?"

"No," I told him, as I tried to catch my breath. "My family's furious. The parade viewing got all messed up, and now they want a refund, and I've been with them for almost twelve hours, and…is there any way…" I trailed off, looking across the bridge at the four empty benches still there.

"How many?" Adam asked.

"Seven." I told him. "But they'll totally stand if they have to. I just need to get them somewhere to watch the parade. I can't have them yelling at the Office because of me!" I took a deep breath and exhaled in the form of tears. Adam threw his arm around my shoulder and pulled me close, not out of solace but to shield me from view for all of the other guests on the bridge. They were here to watch the Christmas Parade, not a hysterical tour guide fall apart.

"Go get them. I'll take care of it," Adam told me, and I nodded into his shoulder. "Quick. You gotta make it back before they close the bridge."

I wiped tears away on the seam of my sleeve and nodded. I gave myself three seconds to collect my bearings, and then I was back, running in front of the Castle, down Main Street, and towards the Plaza Gate. The family was waiting there for me.

"We have to run," I said, panting. "The parade has already started."

"Where are we going?" Mom snapped. I didn't have time for this right now. We had to beat a parade.

"The bridge. Come on. Run!" I took off sprinting through the crowd, and headed onto Main Street again, this time with my own little parade in tow. The family and I ran down Main Street, in front of the Castle, and to the bridge. We hit the bridge just as the announcement came over the loud speaker, announcing that the parade was mere seconds from starting. The family didn't even bother unhooking the rope, they jumped over it and ducked under it and took the benches in the back. I collapsed into Adam's arms.

"Don't worry, it's okay." He said, rubbing my back. "It's just a parade. It's not the end of the world."

"But it was the end of my world!" I cried. My tears were now drowned out by Christmas music filling the air.

"Come on, let's go to the back." Adam let me out of his grasp and moved to the back of the bridge. I turned to follow him, but someone sitting in the front row of the bridge caught my eye. It was dark, so it took me a second to focus on her face, and her hair, and her kind smile as she nodded at me, because she had heard everything that Adam had said to me, and she felt bad for me. It was Snow White.

Not the character Snow White. No, she was going to be passing by us in the parade. It was the actress who portrays Snow White on *Once Upon a Time*, one of ABC's flagship shows. Ginnifer Goodwin smiled at me, like the real-life princess that she is, and at first I thought, oh, that's so awesome, Ginnifer Goodwin's here! Then I thought, oh god, Ginnifer Goodwin just saw me completely and emotionally break down over a parade.

My guests noticed Ginnifer before I did. They couldn't care less about the parade now, they were completely focused on the fact that they were watching the parade with Snow White herself, and that Snow White was watching the parade. Mom completely forgot about the fact that she had threatened to demand a refund for the tour, and that she had completely lost it on me only a half hour prior. None of that mattered because she was ten feet away from a delightfully adorable actress.

Mom was still simmering down as I drove the family back to the hotel. She knew I had cried over the tour, but she didn't feel the need to apologize for her behavior. She told me that, regardless, everyone had in fact had a fun day, and she was thankful for that.

"But if Trevor is standing outside at the valet with that stupid smile on his face, I'm going to punch him," she snarled, as I approached the hotel. Thankfully, Trevor was gone for the night and spared a physical beating from the mom who had just given me an emotional beating.

TWENTY-SEVEN

"Tim, stop poking Sasha," I said, again, for about the fifteenth time that day. Tim was pretty adamant about poking his sister in the arm, though. Like he had been doing since we had picked the family up seven hours ago. I pulled out my Blackberry and sent a message to Abby.

Why are we still in Animal Kingdom?

Do you think they'd believe us if we told them that it was closing now?

It's 4pm.

Do you think they actually know when Animal Kingdom closes?

True. Doubtful the family was keeping tabs on park operating hours, because that's what Abby and I were there for. We were doing one of the rare two-guide tours. These tours required more than ten guests, and it was rare that guests were willing to shell out $600 an hour to be led around the parks. But this family was special. The Orange family had been to Disney many times before and always brought extended family members and always needed two guides. They were a return tour for another set of guides, but those guides opted out of hosting them again. Abby and I couldn't figure out why. The family seemed perfectly normal, most of the time. All families seem perfectly normal.

I was leading the family from the back of the park up to the front, and Abby was bringing up the rear of the group, pushing the stroller with the two youngest girls on the tour inside. While Abby got the adorable three year olds, I got Tim the Terrorizer and his sister, Sasha the Socially Maladjusted. They were odd kids. Tim had no concept of personal space, and Sasha asked the same question again and again until you just wanted to scream YOU'RE ELEVEN YOU SHOULD UNDERSTAND THIS.

Do you think we're going to eat? I'm staaaaarving.

Maybe we can talk them into ending early? Contempo Café? I want cupcakes.

I want pizza.

Pizzafari?

Hell no. I'm not bringing them in there.

Could we squeeze them into Tusker?

We're doing that tomorrow for breakfast.

Uggggggghhhhhhhh.

The Orange family had Abby and I for five days. We started early in the day and we went way late into the evening. They also loved eating, which wasn't a problem for either Abby or I, but we slowly realized we were running out of places to take them to eat. We had already exhausted all of our options in Magic Kingdom and we had only spent eight hours there.

"Tim, seriously, you need to step away," I said to the kid, as he took a big step into my personal space, trying to get closer. He was not a child I'd choose to spend additional time with. Usually I get along with tween boys perfectly because I can talk about video games and superheroes, but Tim was in a complete league of his own. He never had anything to say, and when he had something to say he was usually yelling it. "How about you go walk with your parents?"

He didn't even bother answering me. He leaned forward and poked Sasha in the arm again. Even she wanted him to stop. Sasha took a step closer to me, as if to shield herself from her brother.

"Tim, please," I said, pointing towards his parents behind us. He looked at them, and then he looked back at Sasha and I. I watched the scene play out in slow motion. Sasha, standing slightly in front of me, took a step forward as Tim took a big step towards her. Tim, with all his power as a skinny eleven year old, reared his arm backwards, formed a fist, and then plunged it forward and right into Sasha's stomach. Sasha, being a skinny twelve year old, took the punch hard. It was so loud and hollow I swear birds from the trees flew away, startled by the sound. Sasha flew backwards into me. I wasn't expecting that, so I didn't have time to react properly to keep her from falling. She crashed into me, I stumbled backwards, and she fell hard onto the dirty Animal Kingdom ground.

Everyone reacted at the same time. I could hear Abby scream from fifteen feet behind me. She thought I had gotten punched, and immediately came rushing to my side and grabbed my arm, pulling me away from the violent twelve year old. Tim's dad rushed to him and scooped him up, as he flailed in the air. One of the aunts rushed to Sasha, who was laying flat on her back in Animal Kingdom. We had accumulated the same kind of crowd that a parade normally receives. One Cast Member from a merchandise cart asked if he should call security.

"No, we're fine," Abby called to him, as she continued to drag me through the mêlée.

"I'm fine, I'm fine, it was Sasha." I fought in Abby's grasp.

"He punched her." Abby couldn't believe what she had seen. "We knew he was a little weird, but *he punched her.*"

Sasha, who had really been a mild-mannered kid for the last three days of the tour, sat on a bench in Animal Kingdom and cried hysterically. She had gotten the wind knocked right out of her and the fall to the ground had startled her more than anything else. Her aunt consoled her as she sobbed.

The rest of the family had stopped a few feet behind us. I had been in the lead of the group, so there's no way anyone had missed what had just happened. The other aunt was trying to calm the girls in the stroller down, telling them that everything was okay and that Sasha was only a little hurt. A little hurt? Sasha will probably never recover from this experience.

"How about we take the kids into one of the shops and let them pick something out?" Abby and I turned to see Mrs. Orange standing next to us, as calm as ever. The woman never broke a sweat and everything was always peachy-keen with her. She also loved to shop. "Isn't there a big shop near us?"

"Down by the Tree of Life," Abby told her. "Maybe we should just end for the day?"

"No, lets go to the shop." Mrs. Orange smiled at us. It was a half smile, one where she didn't even bother to smile through her teeth.

Mr. Orange refused to put Tim down as we walked through the rest of Animal Kingdom. He carried him like he was game that had just been shot, slung over his shoulder with his legs high up in the air. I was scared Tim might kick his dad in the face, or worse, a passing guest. But Mr. Orange didn't seem to mind this at all, and I wondered if this was a normal occurrence in the Orange household. Sasha was still crying.

We stopped at Island Merchantile and the girls jumped out of the stroller and rushed inside to shop, dragging their mothers with them. Sasha stumbled into the store, tightly clinging her mother who could be heard saying, "You pick out whatever you want, sweetie!"

"When are we going to get something?" Abby mumbled to me, as she pushed the empty stroller to the side of the building. She leaned against it. "Seriously, what kind of shit was that?"

I shook my head. "I just never thought he would react like that. Completely unprompted! Would it be reason to end the tour if he had hit *me*?"

"Do you want to pretend he hit you?" Abby asked. We both were having the same thoughts about this family. We had been scheduled to be with them for five days, and at the end of day three we wanted to give up. At least we were halfway to the actual conclusion of the tour. The family was just a mess. I had been with messy families before, but none like this. Mr. and Mrs. Orange wandered around in some haze-like state. We weren't told that Sasha hated darkness until after we took her on Haunted Mansion. We had to deal with her freaking out for a half hour while we rode Peter Pan again and again on loop.

I didn't think we could pretend that Tim had hit me, even though we desperately wanted to end this tour. The Office probably wouldn't let us. This was one of those tours where we would feel awful pawning off the guests from another guide. Sometimes it was just necessary to take one for the team.

After a while, when Abby and I realized that the family wasn't coming out of the shop anytime soon, we found two stools and sat down on them. We weren't supposed to sit onstage for any reason, but this was one of those scenarios where the two of us together would be fine. We nestled ourselves behind a closed hair-wrap stand, so at least we were a little bit obstructed. Abby pulled out her phone to text her boyfriend.

I didn't have anyone to text, since I didn't have a boyfriend and I knew that my two best friends were still at work somewhere in the Magic Kingdom. I pulled out my phone and scrolled through new Twitter updates, but nothing exciting was happening.

I heard Mr. Orange approach before I saw him. He came around the corner of the store, still holding Tim tightly in his hands. The boy was thrashing violently, and Mr. Orange motioned to put him down like setting a squealing pig free.

"Are you going to behave?" Mr. Orange asked. Tim nodded. Mr. Orange handed Tim a pair of shoes. Both Abby and I looked down at Tim's feet, to see that he wasn't in fact wearing any shoes. Tim sat down on the ground and put them on.

"That's punishment," Mr. Orange said to us.

"Um," Abby started. "He always has to be wearing shoes at Disney World. It's a policy," she said, struggling for the proper phrasing.

"He's my son. We're looking at reform schools. There's one in Florida." Mr. Orange told us the name of the school and wandered inside with Tim. Abby immediately Googled the school.

"At least eight boys have reportedly died at this school," she said, showing me the news article. "I don't want to be on this tour anymore."

"Do you think we could both get suddenly sick? Something we ate?"

"But we ate with the family. Shouldn't they get sick, too?"

"Abby, I am willing to let you push me into the moat around the Tree of Life. There's a change of clothes in my van, anyway."

Abby mulled this idea over for a moment. It might be the only way to escape.

We spent the next half hour concocting different ways we could end the tour ("Maybe I fell off Dinosaur?" "Maybe I fell into the crocodile river?" "Emotional breakdown during It's Tough to be a Bug?" "Lice?" "2319?") but nothing seemed plausible. We became so invested making up a believable story to get ourselves off of it, that we didn't realize that so much time had passed. Abby suddenly perked up, worried that the family had exited out a different door in the shop, and went rushing in to check on them.

I continued to sit on my stool hidden behind the hairwrap stand and watched guests slowly exit out of the park. It was late in the day, so activities at Animal Kingdom were quickly winding down. Safari was already closed, and there weren't any more shows of Festival of the Lion King or Nemo. Why were guests still even in the park? Animal Kingdom should really be considered a Fun & More ticket option.

"They're still shopping," Abby said, like it was the worst news she could ever give. "Are you hungry?" I nodded. Abby ventured a little ways down the path and returned with two Mickey ice cream bars and diet Cokes. We ate in silence.

In all, Abby and I spent two and a half hours sitting on the stools waiting for the family. I was $300 an hour, Abby was $300 an hour, and together we were $600 an hour. For two hours, $1,200. For two and a half hours, $1,500. We could have bought all of the Mickey ice cream bars in the park and then some for that amount of money. When the family emerged after what felt like an eternity, they had more shopping bags than they could carry and had the littlest ones walk so the stroller could be used as a shopping cart. Abby and I pushed it tandem out of the park, so we didn't have to interact with any of the family. Tim was forced to take his shoes off again, and we wanted no part in that.

When the family returned a year later we opted out of hosting them again. God bless the tour guide who was tasked to them.

TWENTY-EIGHT

A majority of guests told me that I was more than welcome to join them for meals, but often I politely declined. I described mealtime as "family time" and it was usually just as awkward as you're imagining it to sit with a bunch of strangers I had literally met four hours beforehand. Every family asked me the same Disney questions every single time. Sometimes I really wanted to sit behind Brown Derby, completely alone, and eat a bagel and a cupcake from Starring Rolls. It was frequently my only downtime.

If I became attached to the kids I always accepted the meal invitation. Sometimes there were so many kids in a group that they got their own table, and I became Head of the Kids Table, an honor I happily accepted. The kids and I would sit and wait for our meals and do the word searches on the menus with crayons I had in my bag and I never minded that responsibility.

Sometimes if it was raining and I didn't want to have to go looking for food somewhere else in EPCOT, I stayed. Sometimes it was pouring, and I weighed the options of staying with the family I didn't care for, or running through the rain to America quick service, and took the latter. Sometimes it was just worth it to get soaked to eat alone.

And sometimes, I started approaching Teppan Edo in Japan and all I could think about was eating the food inside. Regardless of whether I liked the family or not, or if they had kids or not, I was going to eat in Teppan Edo. I checked the family in at the podium, told the hostess there I would be joining the family, and then returned back to the family to tell them we'd be seated in a moment.

Mom rummaged around in her purse. "Annie, can you do me a favor?" Mom pulled out a long white cord and handed it to me. "Can you go charge my phone for me?"

"Oh, Annie, take mine, too! It's almost dead." The teenage girl handed me her phone. She turned to her teenage brother. "How's your battery?"

"Dead," he said, handing me his phone and his charger.

Dad did the same. Four phones, three different phone chargers. One tour guide to charge them all.

The family was called seconds later and they got up and disappeared from my sight down the long hallway into the restaurant. I stood in the Teppan Edo lobby wondering how many other guests had seen this transpire, and if I was going to acquire any of their phones as well.

I stumbled out of Teppan Edo and down the steep steps to the ground. I walked around the entire Japan pavilion until I found two separate wall outlets, about ten feet apart from each other, and sat in-between the two of them in the Japan loading dock. Countless International Cast Members came over to ask if I was okay, and I explained as best I could that I was doing a favor for my guests. One hospitable Cast Member brought me rice in a take-out container. I sat on the cold ground and ate rice with the provided chopsticks.

An hour later, when all of the phones had at least 50% battery life, I returned upstairs to claim my guests. Mom came down the hallway, grinning because she had just savored a delicious meal at a delicious restaurant.

"It was so funny, Annie, they sat us at a table and there were outlets right next to us!"

"That's so funny!" I said, but it was literally the least funny thing I had ever heard.

TWENTY-NINE

I trailed behind my guests, my nose buried deep into my Blackberry like Belle's nose buried in a book. I watched all 37 guests pass through the back entrance of Tower and I reluctantly followed in behind them. First it was through an entirely white hallway, the airlock of Tower, and then through a door that led out directly next to the PhotoPass view. It was like a giant parade for guests doing the rider swap at the exit.

Hanna gathered all the guests in one giant group. She acknowledged my presence with a wave of her hand. "The elevator will only fit nineteen people. So we're going to have to split into two groups."

No one moved. It might have been the language barrier. Hanna stepped into the group and divided them herself. She beckoned for the first group to follow her. I instinctively stayed behind with the second group.

Hanna disappeared around the corner and through the door located between the two elevator shafts of Tower. It led down a hallway and towards the bypass elevator, or the chicken elevator, or the elevator you take if you're too scared to ride Tower and opt out. It was also the only way to PEP tower; a literal back entrance through the exit.

A coordinator stuck his head around the corner and called me forward. "You ready?" he asked. I moved forward, and my guests followed, all nineteen of them. Someone must have opted to sit this ride out, but I didn't know who. I barely even knew who my guests were.

I grabbed the door and motioned for them to follow the coordinator inside. I counted, seventeen, eighteen, nineteen, they all disappeared down the hallway. One of the last through turned to look at me. "Are you riding?" she asked.

"No, you girls enjoy!" They disappeared. I let the door close behind them and I leaned against the fake brick wall. Defeated. Exhausted. Demoralized.

The coordinator returned to the exit. I recognized him, but I knew him only from the name on his nametag. KYLE. "Are they, um, going to want to ride again?"

"I have no idea. I will pay you a hundred dollars to get me out of here." I said to him.

Kyle laughed nervously. "That bad?"

"I'm serious. I will pay you a hundred dollars if you pretend you didn't see me sneak out of here. Tell them I got sick and passed out or I was abducted by aliens, whatever. Hundred bucks."

Kyle thought I was joking. He laughed again. "Don't think I can do that."

I reached into my bag and pulled out my wallet. I had the cash on me. I had more than enough cash to pay Kyle off with. I pulled out two hundred dollar bills and waved them in front of him. "Two hundred dollars to finish this tour for me. I'm serious."

Kyle looked at the money in my hand. Guests had started exiting out of one of the Tower shafts. He swatted my hand down, to hide the money.

"I don't think you can sell me your tour," he whispered.

"I was never told that I couldn't. Please." I begged. I had never been more serious about anything in my entire life.

But wait. How did I get here? How did I end up at the exit of Tower trying to bribe the coordinator on duty into finishing my thirty-seven-person tour?

There were certain tours that carried a known connotation. As a guide I knew what I was getting into when I was assigned a three-person tour, or a tour that had every single meal planned out for them, or a tour that started late in the afternoon so they could watch the Electrical Parade from the bridge. Then there were the Middle Eastern tours. I had never done one before, but I heard the stories from other guides about tours who came to Disney World with backpacks full of cash and tried to literally buy their way onto re-rides again and again. They came with detailed security brigades and spent an abundant time shopping. I had a clear preference not to do them at one point in time, but there was nothing to save me from this tour.

Once again, I was the last tour guide available when the call came in. The tour was going to need four guides for thirty-seven guests. But, they wanted at least two female guides. So even though I was completely unneeded by the tour, I became the bonus female guide.

There were three boy guides, too. One of them was Andrew, a guide in his mid-30s who was a dad with two kids. Andrew was pretty cool. I liked Andrew. I had never done a tour with him before, but I had seen him enough in the Office and around the parks so I considered him a friend. The other two I did not consider friends. One was a boy named Thomas, who was a French international tour guide who loved the ladies and the ladies loved him. I found him to be bossy and arrogant and we never got along. The other boy was also an international, from Mexico, and his name was Carl and I could only understand him half the time. He spoke in soft, broken English mumbles and came a little too close into my personal space. This wasn't exactly the crew I wanted to spend an entire day with.

The last thing this crew needed was a little Jewish girl from Boston.

We weren't really given instructions for the tour. The coordinator who set it up told us that the guests were foreign dignitaries and one of them "may or may not be a princess". We never actually figured that out. Due to Middle Eastern cultures, we also weren't allowed to ask if any of them were a princess, or actually talk to them. They came with a security detail, and that's who we had to relay communication through.

"Oh, also, please remind *their* security that *our* security will meet them at the entrance to the parks, to check for firearms," the coordinator told us before we headed out. Awesome.

The five of us met at the Office at 9am. We had to pick up the guests at 10:30am, but they were staying far off property so we needed a good amount of time to get there. We all drove away in matching white 15-passenger vans, a small caravan of tired tour guides.

I was the last one out of the parking lot, and the last one to drive down I-4. I watched the white vans drive in front of me, and I tried my hardest to keep up with their speed, but driving those vans above 50mph was like driving a Dinosaur car off-road.

As I drove along a small blue bird slammed against my windshield and I screamed as it bounced off and rolled away. I have no idea if it died, but it left a small circle dust mark that I couldn't get off with windshield fluid no matter how hard I tried. When I met the other guides at the hotel and told them about this, Thomas politely told me, "I think that's considered a bad omen in their culture."

The guest's head of security met us. There were three different security members, two men and one woman. They took us into a side reception room where two things happened: 1. I was frisked by security; and 2. I was asked if I had any firearms on me. I didn't have any firearms, but I did have at least two half-eaten granola bars in my purse.

The Woman explained to us how the day was going to go. Just like the tour coordinator had told us, we were not allowed to talk directly to the guests, and everything had to be relayed through security. The guests wanted to go to Magic Kingdom.

It wasn't really clear how they separated the group, but some got into Hanna's van, and some got into my van, and a few got into Thomas' van, but no one really got into Andrew or Carl's van. I drove to Magic Kingdom in complete silence. I pulled up into Park One and the guests started piling out, heading into the park before I had time to stop them. Hanna went running in to catch them as The Woman grabbed my arm.

"Can we get them water?" she asked.

"Yeah, of course, there's a stand as soon as we enter."

"Is it room-temperature?"

"Uh, the water?"

"They would like room-temperature water."

By this point the boys had showed up with their empty vans. I turned to Andrew, who in my mind, since he was the oldest, was in charge of the tour. He was the designated dad. "Room temperature water?"

Andrew laughed. "It's ninety degrees out. No one is stocking room temperature water.

The Woman was not pleased. "You need to find room temperature water."

Andrew gave me a look. He glanced back at Thomas and Carl collecting their things out of the vans. "I'll see what I can do, but I'm not making any guarantees." He waited for a second, and held out his hand, the universal tour guide sign for, "Please give me a credit card so I can purchase this ludicrous thing for you."

I ran in behind the guests as they moved through Tomorrowland. Hanna sent me a message on my Blackberry.

Space.

I moved through the crowd, half my guests, half other guests in the park, and caught up to Hanna. "So we're just going to put all thirty seven of them on Space?"

"I guess," Hanna said back to me, looking over her shoulder at the parade behind us. "They're not all riding. Did they talk to you in the car?"

"No one said anything," I told her.

"They sort of talked to me. It's one of their birthdays or something, so this is like the birthday present. And the men?" Hanna looked towards the half-dozen men in the group, not counting the security members and the two little boys trailing along. "They're not allowed to ride with the women. Some cultural thing. So, if the men are riding, they have to ride separately."

We made it to the entrance of Space. The Space greeter looked at us with wide eyes. "Uh, how many?" He asked Hanna. Hanna shrugged.

"It'll be a surprise for all of us!" I yelled at him. Hanna went through the queue line and half of the guests followed her. The other half stayed behind and found a place to sit in the shade. I could have stayed out with them, but instead I made the choice to follow Hanna and the guests inside the building. I managed to count heads and discovered that there were twenty-seven people riding, and divide that by six, we were going to need four-and-a-half cars to get all the guests through. Hanna stood at the load area for Space, and I stood down by the exit making sure that everyone getting off knew how to get out.

Somehow Andrew made his way inside the building, and he greeted me at the exit holding a blue merchandise bag. "Water," he said, holding it up to show me its weight. "I begged some Outdoor Foods manager to let me buy two cases of it before it went into the freezer."

He tossed me one and I chugged half of it before the guests got off of Space. Hanna came down once the last guest had been loaded on.

"They want to have lunch somewhere," she said to me, as I handed her room temperature water. She chugged it, too. "One of them mentioned it to me. Where the hell are we going to put thirty-seven of them?" I pulled out my phone and sent a Blackberry message to the other Cast Members in our group. It seemed to be the easiest way to communicate, since we weren't all in the same location.

They want lunch. Where. Open to ideas.

Cosmic Rays.

Not enough money in the world for that. We'd need half the room.

Everywhere is probably booked. It's almost lunch.

Someone call the Office. Thomas, call the Office.

We're heading to Barnstormer.

WHY.

They want "thrill ridz". Barnstormer. Then Thunder?

What about lunch.

Thomas, call the Office.

We're passing Speedway. Meet us at Barnstormer.

I honestly had no idea where the other guides were. Hanna was supposedly with the majority of the group, headed to Barnstormer. Andrew was somewhere with forty-eight bottles of room temperature water. Thomas was maybe calling the Office. Carl was...somewhere.

I raced out of the Tomorrowland Arcade, which doubled as the Space merchandise shop, and ran along the pathway that led from Tomorrowland all the way to Fantasyland. Everyone riding the Speedway saw a little tour guide run, holding her black purse in one hand, half a bottle of water in the other. I wonder what they thought of me.

I managed to intercept Hanna and the guests before they made it to the Barnstormer queue. The Barnstormer area is pretty open, with both queues completely exposed to weather elements and each other. Hanna began herding them into line when I felt a tug on my vest, and I turned to see The Woman standing behind me.

"Can you clear out the line for us?" she said.

"They're going to walk right to the front," I said, pointing at the completely empty FastPass return line.

"The other line. Can you clear it out for us so they don't have to walk alongside other males?"

"The...the standby line?" I stammered. I looked at Hanna standing at the FastPass entrance. She looked at me, confused.

"I don't want them walking through that line so exposed," The Woman said to me. "Could you clear the other line for us?"

"No," I said, without hesitation. I motioned Hanna forward with my hand, and she entered in, the horde of guests following behind her.

"I don't want them walking through that line!" The Woman barked at me.

There are times when I was more than willing to go above and beyond for a tour I really liked. There were certainly tours where I pushed strollers through the rain without an umbrella, or sacrificed my dinnertime to run an errand across property to replace a lost plush toy, or rode Primeval Whirl against my will. If I really liked a family I was totally willing to ride Primeval Whirl if it made the kids happy, even though I got onto that attraction every single time thinking that it might end my life.

I don't want to say that I was culturally unaware of what was going on, but I was. No, I will admit that I didn't have a wealth of information about Middle Eastern cultures and practices, but I knew enough to not be disrespectful. However, here I was, standing outside of Barnstormer, and the head security liaison on the tour had just asked me to clear out an entire queue line so the guests could be comfortable. That seemed disrespectful. No, that downright *was* disrespectful. I wasn't about to go to their home and demand things to be done a certain way; they couldn't come into my World and do the same.

"Unfortunately, there is no chance that is happening," I told her, sternly. "There are guests in that line waiting to ride and I'm not forcing them out."

The Woman was still not happy. She turned sharply away from me and hurried after the guests moving through the line.

> Security woman wanted me to basically evac Barnstormer so the princesses could ride.
>
> Not cool.
>
> They still want lunch.
>
> uggggggggghhhhh.
>
> Called the Office. They can do The Wave. It'll be easy. We'll get them out after Barnstormer.
>
> They want to ride Thunder!

I looked up at Hanna, standing at the load area of Barnstormer. She looked down at me. It was barely noon and we were already defeated.

After an unsuccessful trek from Barnstormer to Thunder, in which the guests opted to ride Splash instead, they all came back to the vans in Park One. Hanna and Andrew took the group of them across the park and back, while Thomas got the vans ready to go, and cooled down to room temperature, and Carl stood around and did nothing. I called the Contemporary and made sure they knew we were showing up in fifteen minutes with almost forty guests for lunch at The Wave. The general manager of the hotel assured me again and again that they would be ready for us.

The drive from Magic Kingdom to the Contemporary took about two minutes, and our vans pulled up at the valet and everyone filed out. One of the boys there recognized me, and came running towards my van.

"We're eating lunch," I called to him through the window. "Do whatever you want with the vans."

I jumped out and went running into the lobby, across the lobby, and down to The Wave. The hostess met me at the podium.

"They're unloading now," I told her, and seconds later my parade of guests passed by, with Hanna in the lead and the security personnel trailing behind. The Wave had managed to clear out a private dining room for the guests, and set a table for forty. However, security quickly informed them that the guests could not all eat together, and there needed to be separate tables to accommodate the males in the group, and also the security members. The Wave scrambled to pull tables apart, and after ten minutes the guests were finally led into their own private dining room. They shut the door behind them.

"Now what?" Thomas asked.

The five of us made ourselves comfortable at the bar where we made friends with the bartender who brought us extra appetizers because we all looked sad and dejected and it was barely 1pm. I ordered a cheeseburger and I ate it like I had never seen food before, and might never see it again. We, collectively as a group, ordered every single dessert off of the menu.

About an hour into lunch we heard the door on the far side of The Wave open and The Woman stuck her head out. She called for Andrew, who jumped to his feet and ran to her. We couldn't hear their conversation, but we could see Andrew's happy disposition slowly disintegrate. He returned back to us like he had just seen a ghost.

"They need a place to pray," he said, like he had just been told he had five hours to live.

No one knew what to say. We all just continued to sit at the bar. I pushed a half-eaten cheesecake around my place.

"Can they do it here?" Carl asked, his first contribution today.

Andrew shook his head. "I asked. They need to pray somewhere else."

This was a common thing to happen at Disney World. I was used to guests from all over the world, and yes, there were areas inside of the parks where guests could pray whenever they wanted to. If a guest came into City Hall and asked for a place to pray, we offered them our VIP Room for as long as they'd like. During training we were told which way pointed west.

It wouldn't be hard for us to load the guests back into the van and take them to Magic Kingdom, but it would be impossible for us to fit thirty-seven of them into the tiny Magic Kingdom VIP room. As soon as Hanna suggested that idea, Andrew shook his head no. "They all can't pray in the same room. Different social classes," he said, like he was suddenly a scholar in Middle Eastern cultures.

"What about here at the hotel?" Thomas asked.

"They need at least three rooms," Andrew started. "I was instructed that they'll need three rooms."

Thomas got up from his seat at the bar and ran back into the lobby of the Contemporary. Andrew followed. Carl sat around for another few minutes, and then got up to go to the bathroom. Hanna and I sat at the bar and ate the remainders of everyone's food, mostly French fries.

It was school vacation time in Disney World, and hotel rooms were a hot commodity at the Contemporary, so no, they couldn't just give us three adjoining hotel rooms. The General Manager laughed when Andrew first requested it. Thomas called the Office. Maybe they could convince the General Manager to give us three hotel rooms for about an hour.

"It's almost check-in time. If we give you three rooms, they have to be completely re-cleaned before 3pm," The General Manager told us, as we huddled around in the waiting area of The Wave. "Are the guests paying for the rooms?"

We looked between one another. There was no way these guests were going to pay for three rooms to pray in. "No," Andrew finally said.

The General Manager looked tired and weary, just like us, but he was managing a hotel with 500+ rooms and a thousand guests, and we were trying to manage only thirty-seven. He had way more reason to be stressed than us. "I'll see if I can find some rooms that requested a late checkout. They might not be clean yet. Would that be okay with your guests?"

"Sure," Hanna said, "We just won't tell them."

The General Manager took Andrew with him into a back room behind the front desk, where they pored over room assignments, trying to find three moderately close to each other with late check-outs. Somehow they managed to find two neighboring rooms in one of the far wings of the hotel. It wasn't three rooms, but it would be good enough, we decided.

Not ten minutes later The Woman stuck her head out of the dining room, again, and informed us that the guests were ready

Chapter Twenty-Nine 129

to go. Andrew explained to her that we would be walking through the hotel to get to those two rooms on the opposite of the hotel for prayer. The Woman did not like that we were making the guests walk through the entire hotel, but there was no other choice. Hanna led them out of the dining room, through the lobby, and to the other wing of the hotel. The guests wouldn't be praying in the A-frame, but instead in the north wing, or the boring wing, of the Contemporary.

Once again, a strange parade proceeded by, with thirty-seven guests, a security detail, and five tour guides, and I was already hungry again. We walked by the pool and into a side entrance of the opposite wing of the hotel. Thomas grabbed the door as the guests piled in, and Andrew called for the elevator. It arrived, and he stepped inside, sticking his arm out to let the guests in, too.

The guests looked from one to another, and silently shook their heads. They looked back at Hanna, standing off to the side, and pointed at her. Then they pointed at me.

Hanna somehow knew exactly what she needed to do. She walked to the elevator, shooed Andrew outside, and took the first group of guests up. I took the second group. Then Hanna took the third, I took the fourth, and this went on for eight trips up and down in a tiny elevator dating back to 1971. It took fifteen minutes.

The General Manager accompanied us on this trek through his hotel, and led us down a long hallway towards our designated rooms. He let the guests inside, showed them that the two rooms were conjoining, and shut the door behind him. He told us to call him when we were done, and disappeared down the hallway.

With all thirty-seven guests crammed into two standard hotel rooms, designed to occupy four at most, we turned the corner down another hallway, where I slumped to the floor. Hanna slumped down as well, pulled out her cellphone, and plugged it into a wall outlet.

I figured we had maybe a half hour of down-time before it was off to the next location, but we really only had ten minutes. The Woman emerged from one of the rooms and asked to speak to Andrew. Alone. They turned down another hallway and I continued to lay sprawled out on the floor in front of some unassuming guest's hotel room.

"We're going to Studios next." Andrew said when he returned to our group. "We should probably go get the cars."

The cars were back on the other side of the hotel. Thomas and Andrew took off running in that direction, as I hurried down to the first floor to await the arrival of the vans. Hanna stayed with the guests, still cooped up in the hotel room, and Carl did whatever he was doing on the tour, which was basically just a silent moral support for all of us. He was doing a great job at it, too.

After two-and-a-half trips, Thomas and Andrew had moved all the cars. Andrew pulled me aside, behind a bush and away from the earshot of Thomas and Carl, who was now eating some trail mix.

"Listen. Don't take this the wrong way. But they want you and Hanna taken off the tour," he said. I looked up at him, and he looked like a dad. A dad who was giving me horrible news, but wanted to make sure that I knew he was there for me no matter what.

"Huh?" I murmured back.

"They don't think you and Hanna are interacting with the guests enough."

"Who is 'they?'"

"Security. They don't know why you're being so distant with them."

"We were told not to talk to them!" I roared back. Thomas looked over at us.

"Security thinks you're not making any sort of effort."

"I was told not to!"

Hanna came out of the hotel, thirty-seven guests in tow. They began climbing into vans and Andrew called Hanna over to give her the good news, too.

"What do you mean we're not being friendly?" she cried. "We were told not to talk to the guests. And now they're mad that we're not trying to talk to them?"

"Basically," Andrew sighed. "They want you guys taken off the tour. I explained that it wasn't possible to do that so late in the day. There's no way another female guide is going to willingly go through this. I'm not going to let any other female guide go through this." Andrew was right. Hanna and I had already suffered through this enough, taking the brunt of the tour, all thirty-seven guests, and their security's ridiculous demands. I would feel bad having another guide take over.

"Let's go to Studios, and get out of there." Andrew patted both Hanna and I on the shoulder, then climbed into his van.

We drove off to Studios and parked in the lot behind Tower of Terror. Which brings me inside of Tower of Terror, and standing at the exit, waving cold, hard cash in front of the coordinator's face, begging him to take my tour off my hands. Please.

But the coordinator politely declined. "Maybe next time?" he half smiled, almost flirting with me.

"I could be dead by then!" I yelled back, loud enough so that everyone waiting in the Tower exit heard me. Carl heard me.

"You okay?" he asked, getting too close to me.

"If you so much as suggest riding Toy Story, I will cut you," I threatened, as the guests began to file out of the elevator shafts and back towards me. Hanna had ridden with the guests, sitting alone, in the back row, all by herself, a blank expression on her face as she plunged thirteen stories down to the ground.

By this point we had thrown all rules out the window. Hanna and I were mentally done with this tour, and I imagined the boys weren't too far behind. We weren't about to walk our guests from the exit of Tower, down in front of Tower, and across the courtyard to Coaster. Instead we cut through the backstage parking lot, and emerged at the entrance to Coaster.

I took one look at the wrapping queue line. The Woman would most certainly protest to being put in that line. "Stay there!" I yelled to Hanna, as I ran up the exit ramp of the attraction, through the merchandise shop, and to a coordinator standing there at the gate.

"Look. I've got like forty guests with me. They're not a PEP, but we've been treating them like a PEP because there are so many of them. One of them might be an actual Princess Sasha. They can't wait in line with males. I wish I were making this up. Can I bring them up the exit?"

The coordinator looked at me. "Are you the guide who just tried to pawn your tour off on Kyle at Tower?" I nodded. "Yeah, sure, bring them up the exit."

I would have given my first born to that coordinator if he asked.

I raced back outside, across the courtyard again, and collected the guests. I marched them up the exit, through the merchandise shop, and down the back hallway leading alongside the Coaster track. Hanna took a head count, and there were going to be twenty five riding. We weren't going to take up an entire car, but we needed two of them anyway. The males couldn't sit with the females and we couldn't load any single riders on. They rode once. We got them off and didn't give them an option to ride anything else. This tour was done.

The boys brought the vans over to us, and the guests climbed inside. I drove in silence back to their hotel. With my big, thick-framed, black tinted sunglasses, none of them saw me cry as I drove down I-4. The guests climbed out of the vans and went inside the hotel without a single word to us. We drove back to the Office. Once inside the Office, Hanna and I cried to the coordinators and I drank a diet Coke in between tears.

THIRTY

No matter how frazzled I looked, or how many children were hanging off of me, or how many bags I was carrying, or drinks I was holding, other Cast Members always used to lean in and asked in a hushed tone, "Who are you with today?" like they imagined my life to be a constant stream of celebrities and their kin.

Most of the time I'd go "just a family!" since that's what most of my tours were. They were just a family. Even when they were a celebrity, they were just a family to me.

However, sometimes the Cast Member would lean in and go, "Who are you with today?" and I'd reply with, "Jonah Hill".

"Ohmygosh, does Jonah Hill want to ride Space again?" the Space Mountain Cast Member asked me as we stood together at the unload dock.

Yeah, Jonah Hill *does* want to ride space again.

When the family got off I leaned into them and whispered, "If anyone asks, Jonah opted out of this ride." And they nodded, not bothering to ask why Jonah wasn't riding again. As they were led up the ramp towards the load area I heard one of the littlest boys yell at the Cast Member, "This made Jonah sick!"

THIRTY-ONE

Once upon a time, I started a five-day tour with a really nice family that was actually super mean. They were a return tour for another guide who said they might be "difficult" but didn't say that they were going to be incredibly inappropriate as we waited in line for Barnstormer one brisk afternoon. Mom, Dad, two kids, two nannies. They all seemed to get along and like each other, but I didn't like any of them. Dad asked me ridiculously inappropriate questions in clear earshot of other guests, I'm pretty sure Mom had a flask of wine in her giant designer bag, and the kids were mean to other kids. Usually I'd just distance myself from the family as much as possible, but the two girls wanted to hang off of me, literally. They both needed to hold my hand, and took my hands, leaving me unable to put a few feet of distance between myself and the family I didn't really want following me into a crowd. If it had just been a one-day tour I would have mustered through. But it was going to be a five-day tour. There was no way I could stay sane for four more days.

The family ate at Crystal Palace, and I excused myself to make a phone call, probably the only time in the history of my tour days when I said I needed to make a phone call and actually made a phone call. I got my comfort food, corn dog nuggets, and sat behind Crystal Palace on the hard pavement ground and called the Office.

I explained as best I could to the coordinator what was happening between me and the guests. I told her some of the things they had said to me, and about other guests in the vicinity of other guests. I told her there was a good chance Mom might be drunk. The coordinator listened to my laundry list of reasons as to why the tour was a grade A recipe for disaster. Much to my surprise, this coordinator completely sided with me.

"I can't make any promises, but I'll see if I can get you off of the tour for the next few days. I'll call you back in a bit," she said, and we hung up.

I ate another cup of corn dog nuggets.

Fifteen minutes later the coordinator called back with good news. She had managed to get their usual guide on the phone, and that guide, a woman by the name of Patricia, had agreed to forfeit her tour for tomorrow in order to take this family, the Pink family. I'd take Patricia's tour.

"Should I tell them I won't be with them tomorrow?"

"No, just drop them off at the end of the night, and Patricia will tell them you're sick or something."

The Pink family finished dinner and decided they were done for the day, even though they had only spent three hours in Magic Kingdom, and one of them was spent eating. I drove them back to the hotel. I said goodbye. I said goodbye forever.

The next morning I arrived to the Office at the same time as Patricia, who apologized again and again for subjecting me to the Pinks. "They're usually not like that. Or maybe I've just learned to tune them out!" She laughed as we collected our vehicle keys and Blackberries.

"Thank you so much, really." I said, giving Patricia a hug. It was customary for tour guides to hug all of the time. Patricia went off to her car, I went off to mine, and I drove to the hotel to meet my new guests.

My new tour family, the Purples, were nice and a little bit quieter. Mom, Dad, a boy and a girl, and then Grandma and Grandpa, the usual. I was told they had lunch at Crystal Palace so we headed off to Magic Kingdom for the day. I parked the vehicle in Park One, and the six of us went into the park. Our first stop, Fantasyland. We were off to ride "small world".

We got all the way to the front of the "small world" and I told the Cast Member there that there would be seven people riding. I like "small world". I also hadn't checked my email yet, so the boat ride would be the perfect time to do so. We loaded into rows and waited for our boat to dock.

"Hot damn, it's the Purple family!" I heard off in the distance. "Honey, you remember Joe, we were college roommates!"

"Hi, Joe!" a woman's voice called back. The Purples turned to wave to the family they knew halfway up the queue. "Look, they have a guide, too!"

I turned around to politely wave, ha ha, it's so funny everyone has a tour guide these days! I raised my hand up into the air but I never got the chance to wave. I looked at the family halfway up the line, quickly making their way towards us.

Out of all the attractions in all of Disney World, the Pink family had to wander back into this one. The one attraction out of all of the parks that tries to show togetherness, and friendship, with a proverb so deep it could end wars if it wanted to. The one attraction that is the literal embodiment of what a "small world" it is we're all living in. It was a world of laughter, and right now it was a world of fears.

Patricia stood with the Pink family in the queue. She looked sick. She looked like she might throw herself into the moat. I contemplated throwing myself into the moat. The Pink family stared at me like they had seen a ghost. I stared back like I couldn't believe this was happening to me, and in of all places, "small world".

"I want to ride with the Pinks!" One of the Purple kids shouted.

"Yeah, Annie, let's wait for the Purples!" Dad said to me, moving out of his loading row. He took a step back against the metal rail.

I literally couldn't form words. The Cast Member loading the boats saw my guest move out, and yelled at us to move back in. I wanted to tell my guests we had to get onto the oncoming boat. We had to avoid the Pink family at all cost. But there was no way I could communicate that to them. Besides, the boats were slow moving. There was a 90% chance that no matter where we went around the park I was going to end up in the same show scene as the Pinks. I couldn't escape. This is probably what Mufasa felt like when the wildebeests started stampeding.

I tried to blend into the "small world" wall as best I could, but it was white and sparkly and everyone could see me in my red vest. The Pinks made their way down the ramp. When they reached the load Cast Member, Mr. Pink yelled, "Fourteen!"

"No, you guys ride without us! Enjoy!" Patricia said, as she reached forward and grabbed my arm, breaking me from my momentary paralysis. She didn't give them time to object, as she dragged me up the stairs behind the "small world" tower and into the sunlight of Fantasyland. I in turn pulled her into the Peter Pan break hallway across the way.

"HOW. WHY. WHAT." I stammered, slumping down into one of the plastic chairs there.

"I'm so sorry! I had no idea we were going to end up at the same place!" Patricia cried, slumping down next to me.

"Not that. *They know each other.*" I took half a dozen deep breaths. I wondered if this is what a panic attack felt like.

"No one could have predicted that." I buried my head into my hands as Patricia rubbed my back. "I'll talk them into leaving the park once they're off. You can have Magic Kingdom today."

I chugged lemonade (it was too early for diet Coke) and Patricia and I returned to the "small world" exit to wait for the Pinks and the Purples. They emerged, laughing and giggling and reminiscing about old times, and the kids held hands as they ascended the ramp.

"Anyway we could change our lunch reservation?" Mr. Purple asked me.

"Uhhhhh..." I stuttered.

"But we have lunch at Hollywood and Vine," Patricia chimed in, as perky as ever, trying not to let onto the fact that the walls were caving in around me.

"We can change that," Mr. Pink said. "I'm glad to see you're feeling better, Annie!"

I nodded.

"How weird is that. Yesterday you were with them, and now you're with us! And look at us, all here together!"

In the remake of the Disney classic *The Parent Trap*, when Dennis Quaid is reunited with his estranged ex-wife she comments that it's a "small world", and he replies, "and getting smaller". That's how I felt.

"It was so nice of Patricia to step in for me," I said, my words staccato as I forced them out. "I didn't feel great last night."

"I'm so happy you recovered so quickly." Mr. Pink raised an eyebrow at me. "I would have hated for these guys to miss out on a great tour!" Mr. Pink slapped Mr. Purple on the back, like old college frat boys. I needed to separate the two of them, before either one of them thought too much into how I had gone from one tour to the other.

"Well, we should probably get moving before the parade cuts us off," I said to the group. It was 10:15am.

Mr. Purple asked me a little while later if there was any way I could make dinner reservations for the two families somewhere in the park, and I nodded like I understood and then consciously forgot about the dining request. There was no way I was subjecting myself to a situation like that again. Patricia sent me a message informing me that they were leaving the park to head to Studios. I continued on with my day as if nothing strange had happened.

I somehow got roped into eating lunch with them at Crystal Palace. I never ate at Crystal Palace while on tour, if only because Casey's was so close and I could smell the corn dog nuggets from afar. But today I was so shaken and rattled, I thought about the air conditioning for forty-five minutes and the fact that their buffet included soft-serve ice cream. I went inside with my guests and sat with the kids while the parents went off to get their meals.

"I'm so glad you're feeling better," Mrs. Purple said once she returned to the table. Surprisingly, none of them picked up on the flawed logic of me being "sick". If I were in fact sick, I would have called in for the Pink's tour, and the Office would scramble for a guide. Patricia wouldn't have been taken off of the tour and put on another just because I was "sick". Because then the Purples would have been without a guide, and once again, scrambling. Also, if I were really sick the Office would still probably make me come in and do the tour even if I had to do it *Weekend at Bernie's* style. It sometimes happened.

I saw the Pinks one more time during their five-day stay at the parks. Patricia was rushing off to parade viewing, and I was strolling along with a new family in tow. She waved to me, but not grand enough to draw attention from others. I waved back, and then ducked behind a trashcan and pretended to throw away imaginary trash, thus causing me to lean down and disappear out of the Pink's sight. They moved into the crowd and I never saw them again.

THIRTY-TWO

If I had known my four-day tour would culminate with me sitting in the Orlando MCO airport food court in full costume, name tag and everything, eating a sad Chick-fil-A sandwich and chugging a diet Coke like I had been parched for days, I probably would have called in sick. I just wouldn't have gotten out of bed.

There was nothing out of the ordinary or strange about the tour. I had been assigned to host a television actor for a few days while he visited the resort area and did a few public appearances and talked to some underprivileged kids, and with the itinerary I had it seemed like it was going to be a very easy four-day tour. William arrived with his wife, Catherine, and both were in their early 60s and didn't really feel the need to trudge through the hot parks just to see the nighttime parade. Catherine just wanted to wander around EPCOT and poke into shops. William would go off to his event early in the morning, and then Catherine and I would wander around EPCOT for a bit, pick William up, the two of them would have a late lunch, then retire early to the hotel.

I found myself bored more than anything else. The two of them wanted to go out to dinner each night, and not an early dinner to accompany their late lunch, but a late dinner usually right around seven or eight. I'd drop William and Catherine off at the hotel around 4pm, and then I'd sit in my car for three hours, with the windows rolled down and the radio all the way up and watch Netflix on my phone.

Don't worry, I didn't do this in the Grand Floridian parking lot. I pulled into the cast parking lot, located across the street, and pulled into an out-of-the-way obstructed parking space so security wouldn't wonder why the tour guide was just shooting the breeze in the middle of the day. Gasparilla's became my haven, and I'd head in there, get myself a flatbread pizza, a diet Coke, a Vitamin Water, a bottle of regular water, and at least two different desserts. Then I'd drive my car across the street, park it, and watch *Parks and Recreation* on my phone for three hours. The car had a USB port, so it wasn't like I was killing my battery. I had tried hiding in the Grand Floridian convention center, but I managed to disrupt one rehearsal dinner and one electronics conference, so sitting in my car seemed to be the easiest thing to do.

I passed three days like this. I watched the entire third season of *Parks and Rec*.

On day four, I arrived at the Grand Floridian nice and early to get William for his last appearance in EPCOT. Catherine was going to stay behind at the hotel to finish packing, so I'd drop William off, double back, get Catherine, and then the two of them would have one last lunch in EPCOT before I drove them to the airport. I checked the status of their flight at 8am before I departed for the hotel. The flight was still on time.

William did his last appearance, Catherine loaded suitcases into my car, and then they had lunch in France while I sat backstage and ate a vanilla ice cream crepe. I collected them from lunch, and the three of us drove to MCO. I pulled into the departure zone, helped them unload suitcases, and Catherine hugged me goodbye. William shook my hand and the two of them disappeared inside.

With the two of them gone, I changed the radio station from the classical music William had requested to the alt-rock Sirius station I enjoyed. I sent a text to my best friend before I pulled away, telling her I was leaving the airport now so we could totally get dinner in two hours if she wanted to.

There was a tap on my passenger window. Catherine stood there, suitcase in hand. "Our flight's been canceled," she yelled at me through the glass.

"What?" I stammered as I rolled down the window. "When I checked in this morning it was on time."

"It's been canceled," she said again. I shoved my phone back into my vest pocket and got out of the car.

"Stay with the car for a second," I told Catherine, as I marched to the curbside counter. The guy standing behind the desk saw me coming.

"The flight was canceled. Technical problems," he told me in a hushed tone, so as to not let other passengers hear.

I groaned out loud. "Can you get them on another flight?"

"It was the last flight back to LA today."

"So...now what?"

The guy shrugged. "You can check with customer service." A sentence that will always frustrate me, because *I was* customer service.

"What's wrong?" Catherine called from the car.

"Is William inside?" I asked her. She pointed through the glass to William, sitting in one of the oddly shaped off-green wicker chairs that MCO had to offer. "I'm going to go park the car in the lot, and I'll be right back for you guys, okay?" Catherine nodded and I jumped behind the wheel of my car.

I pulled into a spot in terminal parking and pulled out my Blackberry. I called the Office.

"The flight's canceled? Why didn't you check the status of the flight before you left for the airport?" the coordinator on the other end of the phone asked me.

"I checked the flight this morning. Everything was fine. I didn't bother checking before I left EPCOT," I told her. "What should I do?"

The coordinator didn't have a good answer for me. She suggested that maybe I try waiting around the airport to see if the flight became un-canceled, like that was a viable option. She suggested I try re-booking them on another flight.

"With my non-existent company credit card?" I asked. The coordinator didn't like that answer.

"William was booked through Disney Travel. We paid for his flight, so just call someone over there. They should be able to rebook him." She gave me the number and I jotted it down on a napkin and stuffed it into my vest pocket, then went running from my car into the terminal.

The time allotment of a tour guide can be divided as:
- 40% waiting for guests
- 30% riding rides with guests
- 15% driving all around property
- 10% avoiding guests
- 5% awkwardly spending time at MCO

I've never spent so much time at an airport before. I never dreamed that becoming a tour guide would have me spending at least five hours at week at MCO, either dropping guests off, or picking guests up, or sitting at the Delta baggage claim hoping that my guests would arrive on schedule. I spent so much time there that some flight attendants actually started recognizing me when I would fly myself. Security recognized me from all the times I had pulled into express parking located underneath the terminal.

By the time I made it inside the building, I had an email from the Office on my phone.

> If they want to stay another night, the Grand will put them up. Just talked to the GM.

It was a Saturday afternoon, and that was probably going to be the best bet. I looked at my watch, and it was almost 4:30pm. Their original flight was supposed to leave at 6. Now they weren't going anywhere.

I found William and Catherine sitting off to the side of the ticketing counter. Catherine waved me over. "Any news?" she asked.

"The flight's been canceled. Technical problems. It was the last flight out for the day. Your room at the Grand is still available, if you'd like to leave early tomorrow morning. I can arrange that now."

"We have a christening to attend in the morning." Catherine told me.

There were very few times I felt like I had no control over the tour. There was the time I somehow wound up hosting nine 11-year olds for a birthday party in the Magic Kingdom, while Mom made business calls on her phone all day. There was the time my guests thought I was giving them a "Christian-based Christmas Tour" of the Magic Kingdom during one of the Christmas parties. There was also the two-guide 16-person tour that only spoke Spanish and I trailed along behind them, having no idea where we were going or what we were doing. But this was the first time I wasn't in control of the situation on Disney property. I had no power at Orlando International Airport. I didn't know what to do.

Catherine could sense that I didn't know what to do. She made the suggestion that we head into the main part of the airport, where we could see the big ARRIVAL and DEPARTURE boards, and maybe William could get something to eat. He hadn't eaten since lunch.

Meanwhile, I thought about the yogurt and banana I had eaten around 9am, and the crepe I had around 2. That's all I had eaten thus far. I didn't realize I was hungry until Catherine mentioned that William might be.

The two of them settled into metal chairs in the open atrium of the airport and I pulled out my Blackberry and typed numbers into the keypad. Moments later I was connected to Kelly, the woman who had set up their initial tickets. I gave her a quick rundown of the situation and ended with, "They need to be back in LA tonight. They have a christening in the morning."

"Jesus Christ, I'm not that magical," Kelly grumbled on the other end. "What am I supposed to do? Charter the Disney One for them?"

"We gotta get them back to LA." I looked over at them. Catherine was completely unrecognizable, unless someone knew she was married to William. William was recognizable. He was a nice man, yes, but he wasn't too fond of the attention that came with being on television. He explicitly told me that he wanted to enjoy time in Disney World with Catherine, not with guests following him asking for autographs. I made him wear a hat and sunglasses as we went through the park, and he went unnoticed. Here in the airport he wasn't wearing a hat or sunglasses, and teenage girls were beginning to notice him.

"I'm going to have to call you back. Let me see what I can do," Kelly said, and then hung up on me. I motioned to Catherine to have William put on his hat and he did so.

Seeing very few options, I wandered over to the customer service desk at MCO. The girl behind the counter was more than eager to help me, and I realized it was because I wasn't a passing tourist. I had a nametag on, just like her.

"Is that…" She started, looking over in William's direction.

"Yes. His flight was canceled. Help?"

"Can I have a picture with him?"

"He's really camera shy. How about you just take a picture from afar here and then tell all your friends you helped him get home?" The girl must have been three or four years younger than I was, and she nodded like the president had just assigned her a Secret Service task. She punched things into her computer.

"There are three more flights to LA today. One leaves in…twenty minutes. The other in two hours, and the last one leaves at 10pm tonight."

"They have to get home ASAP."

"I can't book the flight here. You have to go to the counter to do that."

MCO is probably the worst designed airport ever, in my opinion. It's separated between A and B terminals, and it's gigantic, and there's no easy way to get from one terminal to the other without literally running the full length of the terminal.

My Blackberry rang. Kelly was on the other end. "I can get them on the flight, but it leaves in fifteen minutes." I could see security off in the distance. The really cool thing about MCO is that just like Disney World, the wait times are posted so you know what kind of line you're going to be waiting in. The wait time for security said 20 MINS. I had no idea how to FastPass it.

"We won't make it," I told Kelly. What about the one in two hours?" Kelly typed into her computer so loudly I could hear her keys.

"It's full."

I groaned. I turned back to the girl behind the service counter. "Can you overbook a plane?" She looked at me like I had six heads. You can't overbook Chef Mickeys, but did tour guides do it anyway? Yes. Why couldn't I overbook a plane?

I made my way back to William and Catherine. Catherine was reading a book. "Good news?" she asked happily.

"There's one flight in fifteen minutes, but we'll never make it. The other is in two hours, and it's completely booked." I dropped my head in defeat.

"We need to make it back to LA tonight."

I called Kelly again. "Do you think I could run down to the ticket counter and beg them to bump someone so William and Catherine can get home?"

"I don't know, I'm not there," Kelly told me. She was literally the worst Gary Sinise.

I made the decision to run from the spot in terminal A all the way to the ticket counter in Terminal B, my hair flopping behind me as I hurried down the corridor, past duty-free shops and confused tourists. I arrived at the ticket counter, completely out of breath.

"Is there any way I could get two guests onto the next flight to LA?" I told them William's name, thinking that might help. They might be more apt to take a guest knowing he had Emmy nominations.

The woman behind the counter shook her head. "Sorry, sweetheart! We're completely booked!"

My phone buzzed. Kelly. "Ask them if they'd be okay sitting separately."

Hold on. Lemme just run all the way back to Terminal A.

"Would it be okay if you guys didn't sit together?" I asked Catherine, still deep in her book.

"That'd be fine. Does one of the seats have extra legroom?"

Kelly heard the question through the phone. "Nope." She said into my ear.

"Unfortunately, no." I told Catherine.

"He needs extra legroom. He just had knee surgery, and I don't want his leg going stiff in the air."

"Did you hear that?" I asked Kelly, into the phone.

"No extra legroom," she said. I hung up with her. Turned back to Catherine.

"Is there any scenario where you guys would consider staying the night? I'll take you back early tomorrow morning. With the time difference you should still arrive in LA before the christening."

"We need to be back tonight." Catherine said. She was firm with her words, and I knew I couldn't ask the question again. I had to get them on a flight.

My phone buzzed. Again. Kelly. "Hey, ask the ticket counter if they can bump someone from an emergency exit row. See if you can get seats switched around."

Hold on. Lemme run back to the ticket counter.

"Possibly. But we won't know that till we're boarding!" The woman behind the ticket counter told me. I told Kelly this. I ran back to Catherine and William.

"Do you think it's possible?" Catherine said, turning to look at William, deep in a celebrity magazine. The teenage girl sitting across from him stared at him with wide eyes of recognition.

"I have no idea. But it'll be the only way to get you home tonight."

"Book the tickets."

I called Kelly back. "The tickets are gone now. Someone else bought them while you were running."

"ARE YOU KIDDING ME?" I yelled into my Blackberry. Everyone sitting in the nearby Chili's turned in my direction.

"I'm going to call the service number here," Kelly said. "Maybe they can help." So Kelly had just been sitting by the computer, playing Angry Bird while I ran the terminal twice over. I was on hold with her for about five minutes before she came back. I had started pacing around the airport, in and out of the newsstand.

"So, they can get two tickets. Not together. Not an extra legroom seat. But one of them might be an exit row. They're going to try to switch someone out."

"Buy them. Just do it." I told her. I'm surprised I didn't have a collection of teenage onlookers as well. If William and Catherine didn't get on the flight, I was going to LAX myself.

"You have to go get their boarding passes." She read me the credit card number over the phone. "The flight starts boarding in forty five."

So, one more time, I ran through the airport, darting by suitcases and rolling luggage as I dashed to the ticket counter like my life depended on it. I furiously punched the credit card number into the machine and verified what I hoped was William's personal information. Two boarding passes printed out and I was moving again before they had time to properly discharge from the computer.

Catherine saw me come running towards her. "Do we have tickets?"

"Here, here!" I basically hurdled over a suitcase. "You're not together. And it might not be extra legroom. But it might be an exit row." I handed her the boarding passes as I grabbed her rolling suitcase.

"Honey, come on, it's time to go," Catherine called to William. He opened his eyes. He had fallen asleep. Did he even know I had just run the course of the airport three times?

I led them through the terminal and towards the security checkpoint closest to their gate. Catherine gave me a big hug, and William gave me a firm handshake. "Thanks for everything," he said, as the two of them disappeared into the herd of tourists trying to get places.

I might as well have collapsed on the floor there. I sighed so heavily people around me turned to look at what was going on. I pulled my cellphone out of my pocket. I wasn't on Disney property. I didn't care. Two hours had passed. I felt like I might pass out.

There was a text from my best friend asking me what time I wanted to meet for dinner.

> I'm still at MCO. (I typed back.)

> I don't understand.

> Neither do I.

I stumbled through MCO trying to remember what ticket counter I had parked near. I passed the food court and I saw, like Gatsby's green light, the neon sign of Chick-fil-A. I don't even like Chick-fil-A. But suddenly, that's all I could ever want in the world. I ordered a chicken sandwich, two orders of waffle fries, and the largest diet Coke they had. I sat in a booth in the middle of the food court, all alone, and ate my food like a hungry scavenger. I thought about the etiquette lessons I had been given so long ago, and I wiped ketchup off of the corner of my mouth. This was probably way worse than eating a corn dog at the exit of Jungle.

THIRTY-THREE

I didn't realize my last VIP tours were my last VIP tours until they were over. I had asked for the weekend off to go to a friend's wedding out of state, and she moved her wedding date at the last second to a month earlier. I didn't know you could reschedule your wedding, but I guess you can. I now had a long weekend, and if my mom knew I had a long weekend she'd get mad at me for having so many days off. I called up the Office and told them that I'd be willing to work Friday and Saturday.

Those two tours were the epitome of the juxtaposition of my time as a tour guide. One tour was awful; the other was wonderful.

Two weeks before those tours I had applied and interviewed for a job outside of Disney. While I enjoyed being at Disney, part of me thought that maybe it was time to spread my wings and fly away. Go the distance. Find a new dream. The job told me I would hear back about the position in two weeks, and Friday was the two-week mark. I kept my phone in my vest pocket all day in case anyone called me to give me good news.

Friday's tour was Grandpa and Grandma and two bratty kids, and Grandma and Grandpa had hired me to watch over the bratty kids. That day, I just wasn't feeling the babysitter's role. My mind was elsewhere, and I spent most of the day distracted. I was waiting for a phone call that would hopefully change my life. But hours passed, and I didn't hear anything. It got to be middle of the afternoon and I thought, what the heck, might as well email them regarding my application.

We were eating in Cosmic Rays, and I snuck away from the table, ordered chicken nuggets, and ducked into a custodial closet by the bathroom. I sat on the ledge of the floor-sink and I composed an email on my phone asking if I could have an update on my candidacy.

An hour later I found myself standing in the queue for Pirates of the Caribbean with my guests. I felt my phone vibrate in my pocket. Without thinking I pulled it out, like I had done so many other times on tour, and I read the email. I got so far as "regrettably" when I stopped reading and shoved my phone back into my pocket. We were standing at the cannons in the queue line, the part where you can actually see the boats approaching the loading dock. My guests and I walked down the ramp, towards the boats, and I told the Cast Member that four people would be riding.

"You're not coming?" Grandma wondered. It was clear that she did not want to have to supervise the children herself.

"No," I replied. No explanation. No excuse. Just no. I turned and fought my way up through the queue line, and pushed open a hidden door that brought me back to the courtyard.

I walked quickly from the courtyard, past the merchandise shop, towards the Adventureland pirates bathrooms, past the bathrooms, and came to a stop at the wheelchair exit for the attraction. It's tucked way far off to the side. I pulled out my phone and called my mom.

I was crying before she answered. Not just crying a little, but hysterically crying, gasping for breath, tears streaming down my face, and then the Walt Disney World Railroad rolled by, and all the guests riding the train saw this little tour guide crying hysterically hidden behind Pirates. I was crying so loudly that the coordinator down at the unload area came upstairs to make sure that everything was okay.

Through gasps I told the coordinator I was fine, and he offered to get me a wheelchair to sit on, or something to drink, but I kept on shaking my head "no". It was just one of those times where I couldn't be consoled. I leaned against the wall and slumped down into a heap on the floor. The coordinator stood idly by, just in case I were to throw myself in front of the oncoming Roy E. Disney train.

"Are your guests on the ride?" he asked after a while. I nodded. "If it makes you feel any better, we're at a ride stop. They're not getting off any time soon."

That was the only bright spot to my day. My guests were stuck on Pirates for a half hour, and when they emerged I had cleaned myself up, reapplied my makeup, and you couldn't tell that I had been crying hysterically in a backstage location moments before. They complained about getting stuck on the ride and at such a "bad spot" and wondered if they would be refunded for their trouble. Grandma asked me that question at least two or three times before the end of the day, and I politely ignored her each time.

I was completely removed from this family for the rest of the day, and mindlessly pushed the stroller all around Frontierland, making a stop at Splash and Thunder before the family decided they wanted to do Country Bear Jamboree. I ushered them into the theater and continued to walk right across and exited out. Conveniently, Country Bear Jamboree exits into Pecos Bill's, and I found myself in line ordering my feelings off of the quick service menu: onion rings, sweet potato fries, a root beer float, and a bottle of water. I took my food, pried open one of the exit doors to Country Bears, and sat on the floor in the dark and ate my food, listening to Big Al sing softly in the background.

As if I had timed it, as soon as they emerged from the show the parade was getting ready to step off on a reversed route, so it would be starting right in front of us. The kids wanted to see the show, so I brought them as close to the rope as I could manage, and I stood behind them while Grandma and Grandpa stood in air conditioning three shops down. The parade rolled by and I just stared idly ahead of it, barely registering the dances and the characters and the floats.

The worst part was that everyone in the parade noticed this sad-looking tour guide standing next to the rope, and I swear every single dancer and character came by to cheer me up. I looked up at the float at one point to see Prince Eric waving down at me, and then he formed a small heart with his hands, pointing at me. I managed a half smile at Prince Eric; Prince Eric just happened to be my best friend's roommate.

The tour ended a half hour early. Grandma and Grandpa were over everything at Disney World, and bid me goodbye as soon as the parade passed. They turned and headed into Liberty Square and I made a beeline for Main Street to continue to drown my sorrow in corn dog nuggets. I took my Casey's Corner meal backstage behind the Crystal Palace and ate in silence.

By this time the parade had made its way down to Main Street, and was loudly exiting off. The princess float came around the corner and I saw all the characters jump off. Prince Eric, still clad in his costume and prince wig, spotted me and came over to find me sitting on the bench behind First Aid. I offered him a nugget and he declined. He offered me a hug and I accepted. I wanted to cry into his shoulder, but he was in his parade best, and there was no way I could let mascara tears run down his white shirt. Ariel would be so mad.

Prince Eric asked me if I was okay, and I assured him that I was. He waved goodbye to me and I finished off my lunch, walked across Main Street, got back into my car, and drove to the Office.

I was less than happy to do another tour immediately the next day, but it was a two-guide tour and I couldn't leave the other guide hanging. It was a ridiculously hot day, and when I showed up to meet the other guide, Harry, he apologized about how he was already gross and sweaty.

The family was Mom and Dad, their kids, their adult siblings and their kids, and then Grandma and Grandpa. We had two fifteen-passenger vans and fifteen guests between the two of us. The kids were cute. Harry was an older dad-like tour guide, while I appeared to be a big sister. The young tweens on the tour took to me and asked me to show them how to braid their hair like I had mine done up all over my head, and asked me about boys and nail polish and Disney princes. I showed them a picture of Prince Eric and I, and they fawned over that for two hours.

Though thinking back, I can't remember any of the kids' names.

Toward the end of the day it started to pour and we got trapped inside of Space Mountain. Ponchos and umbrellas were conveniently placed in the van back in the parking lot, and the family made the decision to run for it. I had no choice but to comply. On the count of three we all rushed out of the building and into the puddles of Tomorrowland as we sped towards our hidden vehicles. By the time we reached the cars we were all soaked, but no one seemed to mind too much. I didn't even mind. I now smelled vaguely like a wet dog due to my wool vest, but the kids thought it was funny. I drove them back to the hotel and everyone hugged me as they left. Dad slipped me a few crisp bills and shook my hand, thanking me for such a wonderful day. I watched them enter the hotel and disappear from my view.

Harry and I drove back to the Office and began our after-tour paperwork. I copied our food receipts while Harry turned in the vehicle keys. "It was such a pleasure working with you today," he said, as I fastened the receipts to their copies. "I hope we can do it again soon! You were such an easy guide to work with."

"Thanks," I replied. "Today was fun."

"You bet!" he went in to hug me, then realized how gross and sweaty and rain soaked we were, and stopped. We high-fived instead. "I'm going to request you next time I need a second guide!" Harry winked and left the copy room. I turned in the receipts, said goodbye to the coordinators still working hard at booking dining reservations, and left the Office.

Like Bean Bunny says at the end of Muppet Vision 3D, "What a cute ending."

THIRTY-FOUR

I saw British Jake one more time before I left Disney.

My last day of work was spent at Magic Kingdom doing the Keys to the Kingdom tour. This wasn't by any means a VIP tour; instead, it was a five hour walking tour of the park where I'd point at lampposts and trashcans and describe their place in Disney history. Unlike a VIP tour, the twenty guests on a Keys tour couldn't dictate what we were going to do in the park. I had a set route and a set lunchtime and they had to listen to me talk about Disney for five hours because I had a microphone and they had earpieces. I loved doing Keys tours.

I was trying my hardest not to be emotional about my last tour, since I was trying to make it my Best Keys Tour ever. Everyone knew I was on the verge of hysterical tears at any given second, so they tried to stay away from topics that might upset me, like how I wasn't going to have corn dog nuggets on a daily basis any more. I knew there was only one spot along the tour route that might give me trouble: Haunted Mansion. It's my favorite attraction; it's been that way since I was little. Saying goodbye to it one last time was gong to be hard. I loved talking about the attraction. I loved the history of the attraction. I knew I could talk for hours on end about it, and even though guests asked me to on a daily basis, I kept my Keys explanation down to a solid half hour. That was the only time I might cry.

Haunted Mansion was discussed during a Keys tour immediately after lunch, which always took place at Columbia Harbour House. I had made it in and out of lunch without any tears, and I only had two hours left of the tour. I looked at my looming friend through the Harbour House windows and knew it was time to go. I turned my microphone back on, alerted my guests that we were moving out, and led them over to the Mansion where I poured my heart into the explanation of its history, its design, and its hidden secrets. Then I led the guests inside and I said goodbye to all my friends: not the Cast Members who worked there, but the ghosts, all 999 of them. I somehow made it out of the attraction without crying and I felt on top of the world.

I began to lead my guests out of Haunted Mansion and through the throngs of guests hanging around in the area. I was crossing back in front of Harbour House when I heard someone call my name faintly off in the distance.

"Princess Annie! It's Princess Annie!"

I turned to look through the crowd and I spotted him: British Jake and his whole family. British Jake sat on his father's shoulders, and the whole family waved to me. I waved back, excitedly. Jake's dad leaned down, and Jake jumped off. He came running towards me. I knew there was only one thing that was going to happen, so I reached around and muted my mic so none of the guests would hear what was about to happen.

British Jake jumped into my arms and it was the most perfect moment. I told him that I had missed him and he told me he was so glad to see me again. I knew it was probably going to be the last time I saw him, ever. His dad came over to collect him, hugging me too, and I hugged British Jake's dad right back. I waved goodbye to him, and I silently cried behind my black sunglasses as I led my Keys tour toward The Hall of Presidents. That's all the time I gave myself to cry. I had decided against telling this Keys tour that it was going to be my last tour ever, and I wanted to keep it that way. They didn't need to know that I only had two more hours left to be a Cast Member.

I wondered if that's what Peter Pan felt like when he dropped Wendy off in her London home. Wendy was just going to go off and grow up without him, like Jake would do without Princess Annie. We reached the Hall of Presidents and I turned my mic back on. I still had a tour to finish.

EPILOGUE

You could say I had a series of unfortunate events befall me during my last summer at Disney. One thing led into another, and that snowballed into something else, and I felt like I had senioritis for a fixed term that didn't have an end date. Like when Belle is singing her little princess heart out about wanting "adventure in the great wide somewhere!"—that's how I felt. But every time I tried to break into song on Main Street I was told to get back to work. I told my managers that, just like Rapunzel, I needed to go out and see those floating lanterns and find a new dream, and one of my managers asked, "Who?"

The day I arrived at Disney I told myself I would leave when everything began to lose its magical luster. I knew the sheen was starting to tarnish around me, and I wanted to hold on to what I still had. I thought about what it was like to be a guest and I wanted that feeling back again. I didn't want to have to stress about reversed parade routes, and refurbishments, and downtimes, weather, gluten-free dining choices, kosher dining choices, and rides that didn't have any hippos because little Sally was terrified of them. I wanted to walk down Main Street again and see the Castle situated at the other side and remember what it was like to see that for the first time. I didn't want to see it any more and think about all the times I had been yelled at in front of it.

There is something absolutely magical about Disney, and I thought about my future children and how I wanted to take them to Disney one day and show them this magical place. I felt like I needed to leave to preserve that magic.

The weird thing about leaving Disney is that you never actually leave it. It's like the Ghost Host who manically laughs at the end of Haunted Mansion, "and a ghost will follow you home!" The Ghost of Disney followed me home.

I can't go a single day of my life without seeing a Mickey Mouse keychain, or a Mickey Mouse antenna topper, or seeing a little kid wearing a Rapunzel shirt, or passing a boy clutching a Woody doll. Disney is everywhere. I can't even go to the gym without someone two treadmills down from me sporting a runDisney shirt. When

I get stuck in traffic, without fail, they'll be a mini-van in front of me with a stick figure family sporting Mickey ears.

I guess you can take the girl out of Disney but you can't take the Disney out of the girl.

And yes, I miss corn dog nuggets every day of my life; I don't miss waiting in the line at Casey's Corner during the parade.

My wish is that I one day become wealthy enough to hire my own VIP tour guide for four days, because I will be the best tour guest *ever*. I won't ask to feed a giraffe, and I won't yell at the guide because they accidentally forgot to book dinner in Italy. I will, however, insist on four different guides for each day. And I plan to thank them all differently. One guide will receive a thick wad of cash. One will receive a stack of gift cards. The third will probably get like some physical gift, maybe like a small kitchen appliance or an Xbox, or something like that. The fourth will get nothing, but I'll mail them an adequate check in a week.

Why?

Because I just want to see how a new generation of tour guides squirms under the pressure of what to tell the Office they had been gifted for tax purposes. Seriously, how is one of them going to declare a KitchenAid mixer? I guess you could say that's my new Disney dream.

About the Author

Annie Salisbury spent 1,164 days at The Walt Disney World Resort and probably ate about 7,000+ corn dog nuggets from Casey's Corner in The Magic Kingdom. In contrast, she has never eaten a Turkey Leg. Her favorite attraction always has been, and always will be, The Haunted Mansion. She still remembers what it was like before the invention of FastPass, and thinks of that time as the good old days.

She has a fancy degree in Film & Television and looks forward to using it one day. She currently lives in Massachusetts with her family, where she is enjoying her newly earned non-Disney Look freedom. Annie would like to thank her fishy, her buddy, her princess, and Scotty.

About the Publisher

Theme Park Press is the largest independent publisher of Disney and Disney-related pop culture books in the world.

Established in November 2012 by Bob McLain, Theme Park Press has released best-selling print and digital books about such topics as Disney films and animation, the Disney theme parks, Disney historical and cultural studies, park touring guides, autobiographies, fiction, and more.

For more information, and a list of forthcoming titles, please visit:

ThemeParkPress.com

More Books from Theme Park Press

Amber Earns Her Ears

Ever imagine what it would be like to work as a Cast Member at Walt Disney World?

Amber Sewell tells the sweet and the sour of her two "semesters" in the Disney College Program, working and playing and crying and eating at the happiest place on earth.

Foreword by Lee Cockerell.

ThemeParkPress.com/books/
amber-earns-her-ears.htm

The Unofficial Story of Walt Disney's Haunted Mansion

Welcome, Foolish Readers!

Haunted Mansion expert Jeff Baham recounts the colorful, chilling history of the Mansion and pulls back the shroud on its darkest secrets in this definitive book about Disney's most ghoulish attraction.

Foreword by Rolly Crump.

ThemeParkPress.com/books/
haunted-mansion.htm

More Books from Theme Park Press

Two Girls and a Mouse Tale

Doubling down on Disney.

Two girls from Colorado spend a year in the College Program at Walt Disney World, balancing pixie dust with reality bites, as they spin magic for guests in the parks, but can't talk their roommates into keeping the apartment clean.

ThemeParkPress.com/books/two-girls.htm

Vault of Walt: Volume 2

Jim Korkis goes back into the Vault of Walt for a second super-helping of unofficial, unauthorized, uncensories Disney stories never told.

In this volume, Korkis tells of the seven Snow Whites, the birth of the Jungle Cruise, Walt's nasty feud with *Mary Poppins* author P.L. Travers, and over two dozen more tales.

Foreword by Lou Mongello.

ThemeParkPress.com/books/vault-walt-2.htm

More Books from Theme Park Press

Service with Character

Disney goes to war!

As Hitler's tanks rolled across Europe, the U.S. government informally drafted Walt Disney. David Lesjak chronicles those dark years, when the Army took over the Disney Studios and even Donald Duck went to work for Uncle Sam.

> ThemeParkPress.com/books/
> service-character.htm

The Book of Mouse

When a mouse as famous as Mickey turns 85 years old, he has lots of stories to tell.

In this comprehensive "biography" of Mickey Mouse, Jim Korkis tells all of those stories, and more, including plenty of "Mouse-ka-Tales" and an annotated filmography of Mickey's cinematic career.

> ThemeParkPress.com/
> books/book-mouse.htm

Discover our many other popular titles at:

www.ThemeParkPress.com

Printed in Great Britain
by Amazon